THE CATHOLIC UNIVERSITY OF AMERICA
CANON LAW STUDIES
No. 107

CANONICAL PROVISIONS FOR CATECHETICAL INSTRUCTION

AN HISTORICAL SYNOPSIS AND COMMENTARY

Submitted to the Faculty of Canon Law of the Catholic University of America in Partial Fulfillment of the Requirements for the Degree of

DOCTOR OF CANON LAW

BY

RAYMOND J. JANSEN, A.B., S.T.L., J.C.L.,
Priest of the Diocese of Winona

THE CATHOLIC UNIVERSITY OF AMERICA
WASHINGTON, D. C.
1937

Nihil Obstat:

VALENTINE T. SCHAAF, O.F.M., J.C.D.

Censor Deputatus.

Washingtonii, D. C., die XXVI Aprilis, 1937.

Imprimatur:

✠ FRANCIS M. KELLY, D.D.,

Episcopus Winonensis.

die IV Maii, 1937.

Printed by

THE PAULIST PRESS

New York, N. Y.

TO MY MOTHER

TABLE OF CONTENTS

PAGE

CHAPTER V

FOREWORD

In recent years the importance of the ministry of catechetical instruction has been repeatedly emphasized. Pope Pius XI, by a *motu proprio* of June 29, 1933, established a special office in the Congregation of the Council to which the task of caring for religious instruction throughout the universal Church was entrusted. From time to time since then the Holy See has issued several decrees bearing on many aspects both of the obligations and of the organization of the teaching of Christian doctrine. A need was therefore felt to explain these decrees in their relation to the legislation of the Code with the hope that the explanations thus given might serve a useful purpose in the enactment of particular legislation.

The first part of this dissertation is historical. Its purpose is to trace the manner in which the Church, through her legislation, has fulfilled Christ's injunction "to teach all nations." The method employed has been demonstrative, namely, to show the nature of this legislation in a manner sufficient to indicate its development as well as the changes that have occurred until its present form in the Code. A commentary of the various canons relating to catechetics follows. These define the various duties of local ordinaries, pastors, and parents or those who hold the place of parents, and for the most part are general in nature. The reason for this is that instruction must be adapted to conditions as they exist in various localities. Attention has also been given to those enactments of the Plenary Councils of Baltimore which are still in force in the United States. In conclusion, three supplements are added. The first lists the indulgences and privileges which the Holy See has granted to those who engage in teaching Christian doctrine. The second is a discussion of the question of religious instruction in the United States from a civil-law point of view. The third is the suggested constitution for the organization of parish units of the Confraternity of Christian Doctrine as approved by the Holy See.

The writer wishes to take this occasion to express his gratitude to His Excellency, the Most Rev. Francis M. Kelly, D.D., Bishop of

Winona, for the opportunity afforded for advanced study. He acknowledges with gratitude the helpful direction of the Faculty of the School of Canon Law. He likewise wishes to thank the Rev. Francis H. Greteman, S.T.L., J.C.L., for his kind and generous assistance in the preparation of this dissertation, and the librarians of the University for their many favors.

CANONICAL PROVISIONS FOR CATECHETICAL INSTRUCTION

CHAPTER I

ORIGIN AND DEFINITION OF TERM

By the divine ordination of Jesus Christ, the Church is vested with a twofold power, namely, of Order and of Jurisdiction. Each has for its purpose the sanctification and salvation of men. The immediate object of the power of Order is the administration of the sacraments and sacramentals (*potestas ministrandi*); the power of Jurisdiction, on the other hand, is concerned with the guidance and government of the members of the Church (*potestas regendi*). As such it comprises a double function, government (*imperium*) and teaching (*magisterium*).[1]

It is with the teaching office of the Church that catechetical instruction is associated. Since the free coöperation of men is required to participate in the fruits of the Redemption, it is necessary for them to know the means that the Teacher of mankind established for this participation.[2] For this reason the Church exercises her important duty of preaching the evangelical doctrines to all men as commanded by Christ and the Apostles.[3] Among the means chosen, that of catechizing is the most fundamental. Rightly can it be said that this obligation springs directly from the divine law.

The Church, in the present law of the Code,[4] has explicitly determined the means by which the divine law is to be fulfilled. Among these, the first is that of preaching the word of God,[5] which includes the triple function of catechesis, sacred eloquence, and missions. Therefore, at the outset, two things need to be made clear, namely, the introduction of the word *catechesis* into christian terminology; and its present meaning in the law.

Etymologically, the word *catechesis* is derived from the Greek simple verb ἠχεῖν meaning to sound, to ring out, and κατά intensive

[1] Ottaviani, *Institutiones Juris Publici Ecclesiastici*, I, 245.

[2] Dieckmann, *De Ecclesia*, II, 1.

[3] Matt. xxviii. 19; 2 Tim. iv. 2; Rom. x. 14.

[4] Codex Juris Canonici, Lib. III, Pars IV, *De Magisterio Ecclesiastico*.

[5] Canons 1327-1351.

meaning down, down from. Thus the compound κατηχεῖν signifies to speak from an elevated standpoint, to sound from above. In a figurative sense the word received among the Greek profane writers, the meaning of instruction, especially by word of mouth; that is, the children in school were instructed by making them "sing out" in chorus the answers to the questions asked by the teacher.[6]

Christianity early adopted the word κατηχεῖν, Latin *catechizare* to signify the instruction to be given to the converts to Christianity. Evidences for this meaning are found in the New Testament, *v. g.*, Luke i. 4: ἵνα ἐπιγνῷς περὶ ὧν κατηχήθης λόγων τὴν ἀσφάλειαν in which the evangelist expresses to Theophilus his purpose in writing, namely, to narrate those truths in which he had already been instructed; Acts of the Apostles xviii. 25: οὗτος ἦν κατηχημένος τὴν ὁδὸν τοῦ κυρίου where Apollo is described as one already instructed in the Lord; the first epistle to the Corinthians xiv. 19: ἵνα . . . ἄλλους κατηχήσω where St. Paul uses the term in the sense of instructions; also in his epistle to the Galatians vi. 6: κοινωνείτω . . . ὁ κατηχούμενος τὸν λόγον τῷ κατηχοῦντι . . . St. Paul again uses this term in the sense of instruction to be imparted.[7] The term was also used by both the Greek and Latin Fathers.[8] Tertullian was the first Latin writer to use *catechizare* in the meaning of "to instruct orally in the Christian Faith," and St. Augustine the first to use the word "catechismus."[9]

Although catechesis, as employed by the Church, has always signified instruction, the comprehension of the term has not always been

[6] Liddell-Scott, *Greek-English Lexicon,*—under κατηχέω.

[7] The exact meaning of this text is disputed: "According to some, the catechumen should try to participate in the spiritual and intellectual possessions of the catechist; according to others, the catechumen should share with his catechist the temporal goods which he possesses in exchange for the spiritual goods which he receives from him. . . ." Prat, *The Theology of St. Paul,* tr. by John L. Stoddard, II, 29.

[8] For example, Clement of Alexandria, ὡς κατηχοῦνται οἱ ἐξ ἐθνῶν ἰδιῶται *Strom.,* 6, 15—*MPG,* IX, 341; St. Cyril of Jerusalem, *Catechesis—MPG,* XXXIII, 367-1128; St. Augustine, *De Catechizandis Rudibus—MPL,* XL, 309-345.

[9] Tertullian, *De Corona Militis,* cap. 11—*MPL,* II, 92; St. Augustine, *De Fide et Operibus,* cap. 13—*MPL,* XL, 210.

the same. From the earliest days of the Church to the decline of the catechumenate, it signified the simple instruction of those totally ignorant of the truths of Christianity. From the decline of the catechumenate to the Council of Trent, the term is not used frequently in conciliar enactments.[10] After the Council of Trent, the term was extended to include not only the subject-matter taught, but also the additional elements of persons taught, those whose obligation it was to teach, and the time and place of this instruction.[11] It is of importance, therefore, to fix the signification of the term as used in the Code of Canon Law.

The essential element is instruction, oral and methodical, adapted to the mental capacity of those being instructed.[12] From this point of view, it is distinguished from sacred eloquence (*concio*) by the immediate end intended. While the former educates the mind to the things previously unknown, the latter presupposes this knowledge in order to arouse to further action. It is distinguished from missions (*missio*) in as much as the latter are concerned with prolonged meditation on eternal truths in order to effect a deeper and more fervent Christian life.[13] The object of instruction comprises, first, those truths which must be explicitly believed by all Christians; second, those actions which must be performed according to the precepts of God and of the Church; third, that the sacraments must be

[10] During the middle ages, the term *catechismus* was applied to instruction in a wider sense, namely, to the liturgical function of the profession of faith made before baptism (Göbl, *Gesch. der Katechese,* p. 5; Schmalzgrueber, *Jus Universum Ecclesiasticum,* lib. IV, tit. XI, n. 59). As a consequence, it was allowed to have a sponsor hold the infant at baptism and one to make this profession of faith, although this was not the common practice (C. 100, D. IV, *de Cons.*). From this an impeding impediment to marriage arose between the infant, the parents, and the sponsors, because of the spiritual relationship thus existing between them (C. 5, X, *de. cognat. spirit.*, IV, 9; c. 2, IV, 3 in VI°). This was abolished by the Council of Trent (Sess. XXIV, cap. 2, *de Matrim*), and likewise the use of the term *catechismus* as applied to this profession of faith.

[11] Wernz, *Jus Decretalium,* III, 35; Hezard, *Histoire du Catéchisme,* p. 1.

[12] "Catechismus graece, latine dicitur instructio, unde catechizare, id est instruere." Glossa in c. 52, D. IV, *de cons.*; Vermeersch-Creusen, *Epitome Juris Canonici,* II, 409.

[13] Blat, *Commentarium textus Codicis Juris Canonici,* III, 252.

received; and finally, the things to be hoped for. Pius X, in his encyclical letter *Acerbo nimis* has accurately summed up the meaning of catechetical instruction thus:

> Perchance there are some who, desirous of saving themselves trouble, are willing to believe that the explanation of the Gospel may serve also for catechetical instruction. The error of this must be apparent to all who stop to think for a moment. The sermon on the Gospel is addressed to those who may be supposed to be already instructed in the rudiments of faith. It is, so to say, the bread that is broken for those who are grown up. Catechetical instruction, on the other hand, is that milk which the Apostle St. Peter wished the faithful to yearn after in all simplicity like new born babes. The task of the catechist is to take up one or other of the truths of faith or Christian precepts and explain it in all its parts; and since the scope of his instruction is always directed to amendment of life, he should institute a comparison between what is required of us by our Lord and our actual conduct.[14]

Therefore, besides the immediate end of educating the mind, there is the ultimate end to be acquired, namely, living according to the truths learned.[15]

[14] "Non enim fortasse desunt, qui minuendi laboris cupidi, persuadeant sibi homiliam pro catechesi esse posse. Quod quam putetur perperam consideranti patet. Qui enim sermo de Sacro Evangelii habetur, ad eos instituitur, quos fidei elementis imbutos iam esse oportet. Panem diceres qui adultis frangatur. Catechetica e contra institutio lac illud est quod Petrus Apostolus concupisci sine dolo a fidelibus volebat, quasi a modo genitis infantibus—hoc scilicet catechistae munus est, veritatem aliquam tractandam suscipere vel ad fidem vel ad christianos moros pertinentem, eamque omni ex parte illustrare. Quoniam vero emendatio vitae finis docendi esse debet, oportet catechistam comparationem instituere ea inter quae Deus agenda praecepit quaeque homines reapse agunt . . ."—Pius X, litt. encycl„ *Acerbo nimis,* 15 April, 1905, n. 12—*Fontes,* n. 666.

[15] ". . . therefore the teaching which we give them, if it only instructs them, it is not enough, we must add to it exhortations which touch them, examples which persuade them, practices which please them, pious exercises which make them better. We must improve their character, correct their faults, strengthen their wills, enlighten and rectify their conscience, ennoble their sentiments; in a word, we must lift their whole soul up, even to God." Dupanloup, *The Ministry of Catechising* (tr.), p. 3.

To sum up: catechesis may be defined as oral instruction, given in a methodical manner and accommodated to the mental capacity of the auditors, in the truths of faith and morals in order that they may learn those things which must be expressly believed and professed by a Christian and which they must carry into practice during life.

CHAPTER II

HISTORICAL SYNOPSIS

SECTION 1. CATECHETICAL INSTRUCTION DURING THE FIRST FIVE CENTURIES

MANY and severe were the difficulties that faced the Church in her beginning and early development. The exacting practices and beliefs of paganism on the one hand, and on the other persecutions and heresies proved to be obstacles to her growth. Nevertheless with a courage inspired by the Spirit of Truth the Apostles and their successors labored valiantly in spreading the Gospel of Christ. The final success of their efforts was due, in no small part, to the thoroughness in which the first members of the Church were instructed. Thus from the very beginning has instruction in the truths of faith been one of her outstanding characteristics.

ARTICLE 1. AT THE TIME OF THE APOSTLES

Sacred Scripture, in the concluding accounts of the four Gospels and the beginning of the Acts of the Apostles, refers in a most striking manner to the complete establishment of the teaching office that Christ commissioned to His Church.[1] The fact, however, that instruction paralleled the preaching of the Apostles is a matter of deduction. St. Luke's Gospel is addressed to Theophilus in order that he might "know the verity of those words in which he had been instructed."[2] St. John writes his Gospel to his companions who were familiar with the life and works of Jesus. Evidences of a meager instruction are found also in the Acts of the Apostles.[3] Three reasons point to a more thorough instruction that soon developed. In the first place, it is the common opinion of scholars that religious instruc-

[1] Matt. xxviii. 19, 20; Mark xvi. 20; Luke xxiv. 53; John xxi. 17; Acts ii. 6 ss.

[2] Luke i. 4.

[3] Acts viii. 37.

tion was necessary as a basis for understanding the Epistles of St. Paul; in other words, the neo-Christians had already been instructed in the common elements of the Christian Faith.[4] Secondly, St. Paul himself acknowledges the activity of teachers other than the Apostles.[5] Finally, the faith of the neophytes was threatened by heresy so that further instruction became necessary; the union of Jewish theology and Greek philosophy was producing various disputes, each school holding out promises to gain disciples. Further indication of defection from the Faith is also given by St. Paul.[6] Therefore it is a safe conclusion to hold that catechetical instruction was provided during the time of the Apostles, and as such is rooted deeply in the foundation of Christianity.[7]

Article 2. The Development of the Catechumenate

The early discipline of the Church was concerned primarily with a careful and adequate preparation for the reception of the sacrament of Baptism. To this end, the institution of the catechumenate developed gradually. That it had its beginnings with St. Paul appears to be a safe conjecture from the outlines of a program as found in the Epistle to the Hebrews,[8] the first Epistle to the Corinthians,[9] and the Epistle to the Colossians.[10] However, in the apostolic age, the catechumenate as such did not exist because such an institution could be founded only in a well-organized Christian community.[11] How soon and how intimately this organization grew together is shown by the Christian writers and Fathers of the Church.

Among the early documents that indicate its beginning is the *Didache*. That this seems to have been intended for catechetical

[4] Prat, *The Theology of St. Paul,* II, 28.

[5] Gal. i. 9: "As we said before, so now I say again: if any one preach to you a gospel besides that which you have received, let him be anathema." 1 Cor. xiv. 37: "If any seem to be a prophet, or spiritual, let him know the things that I write to you, that they are the commandments of the Lord."

[6] Hebrews v. 11; Gal. vi. 6, 7.

[7] Mayer, *Geschichte des Katechumenats und der Katechese,* p. 11.

[8] Hebrews vi. 12.

[9] 1 Cor. xi. 23.

[10] Col. iii. 8-12.

[11] Mayer, *Gesch. des Katechumenats,* p. 9.

instruction is gathered from its content, namely, of moral conduct, church discipline, and eschatology; [12] in addition chapter fifteen indicates that the offices of bishops and deacons were to offer Christian sacrifice and to instruct the faithful.[13] Another indication of its existence is in the first *Apologia* of St. Justin Martyr (100/10-163/7) wherein a period of instruction and examination is mentioned.[14] *The Clementine Recognitions* [15] also indicate a time needed for instruction. Origen (185/6-254/5) indicates two grades in the catechumenate, namely those who were the catechumens proper, and the *competentes.*[16] Hence by the time of the third century, this institution of probation and instruction for Baptism was fully developed. It is generally admitted [17] that there were two stages in the catechumenate, that of probationer and that of approved catechumen.[18] The latter were those admitted to preparation for Baptism, which included the instruction technically called *catechism.* This institution of the catechumenate became universally established in the Church and flourished until about the sixth century.[19]

It is in relation to this institution of the catechumenate, established as it was by custom, that the first instances of ecclesiastical legislation are found which pertain to catechesis. Instances of such can be classified as follows: (A) Certain conditions of admittance were required. According to the *Apostolic Constitutions* [20] the candidate for admittance had to present himself to the deacon or to the bishop, or if the bishop so ordered, to a priest. These latter in turn investigated the motives of the applicant, the present condition of

[12] Otten, *A Manual of the History of Dogma,* p. 62.

[13] C. 15: "Constituite igitur vobis episcopos et diaconos dignos Domino . . . vobis enim ministrant et ipsi ministerium prophetarum et doctorum." Funk, *Patres Apostolici,* I, 32.

[14] *Apologia Prima Pro Christianis,* cap. 61—*MPG,* VI, 420.

[15] *Recognitiones S. Clementis Romani,* lib. III, cap. 49—*MPG,* I, 1311.

[16] Origen, *Contra Celsum. MPG,* XI, 892.

[17] Concerning the number of grades in the catechumenate, there is lack of agreement among those who have studied this institution more thoroughly. For a further discussion, *cf.* Devoti, *Institutionum Canonicarum,* Lib. IV, tit. II, no. 29, 30.

[18] Reichel, *A Complete Manual of Canon Law,* I, 34, 35.

[19] Poulet, *A History of the Catholic Church,* I, 262.

[20] *Constitutiones Apostolorum,* VIII, 32—*MGP,* I.

his life, and the attestation of witnesses. That this came to be the general practice is evident from the fact that when Christianity was given its freedom and became the religion of the world, pagans in great numbers joined the Church, many not being led by the highest of motives. Such a discipline of examination, therefore, became necessary.[21] Persons whose worldly positions argued against their persevering were accepted only on certain conditions; for example, slaves were admitted only if they had a Christian master.[22] Moreover to certain classes admittance was prohibited, for example to women of doubtful character, and those associated with the pagan theater and its practices.[23] (B) Certain regulations were also placed concerning the length of time of the catechumenate. This period, however, varied with different places and persons. The Council of Elvira (305/6) for example, set the length of probation at two years for those who had good witnesses.[24] The Council of Nice (325) anathematized the practice of receiving pagans into the Church after a short instruction.[25] Moreover it set the time at three years.[26] The same length of time seems to be required [27] by the Apostolic Constitutions. Such regulations crept into the law of the Empire at the time of Justinian. He set the period at two years; in addition, he gave the Nicean enactments the force of empirical legislation.[28]

[21] Mayer, *Gesch. des Katechumenats*, p. 40.

[22] Council of Elvira (305/6), c. 44—Hefele, *History of the Christian Councils*, I, 155.

[23] Council of Elvira (305/6), c. 66—Hefele, *Hist. of Christian Councils*, I, 165; 3 Synod of Cathage (397), c. 86—Hefele, *op. cit.*, II, 417.

[24] Canon 42: "eos qui ad primam fidem credulitatis accedunt, si bonae fuerint conversationis, intra biennium temporum placuit ad Baptismi gratiam admitti debere."—Hefele, *Hist. of the Christian Councils*, I, 155.

[25] Canon 2—Hefele, *History of the Christian Councils*, I, 377.

[26] Canon 14: "de catechumenis et qui lapsi visum est et sanctae et magnae synodae, ut ii tribus tantum annis audientes, postea orent cum catechumenis."—Mansi, II, 674.

[27] *Const. Apostolorum*, VIII, 32—*MPG*, I, 1127.

[28] ". . . Bene autem se habere videtur, ut non protinus recipiantur cum ad immaculatum baptisma accurrant, sed cum quadam observatione et institutione per sufficiens tempus facta. Dicimus autem eos quidem qui bonam doctrinam omnino percipiant per duos annos institui et scripturas quoad fieri potest discere, ac tum demum ad sanctum redemptionis baptisma accedere, tanti temporis paenitentia veram redemptionem lucratos." (N. 144, 2, 3.); (N. 131, 1.)

There were also regulations relative to the ceremonies, preparatory to Baptism. These concerned solemn exorcism by a presbyter as well as by an exorcist; prayer and fasting; and learning and confessing the faith.[29] Since these pertain to the sacrament rather than to instruction, they are omitted.

Relative to this legislation, two facts are outstanding. The first is that there appears to be no express regulation concerning those who were to instruct and the nature of this obligation. That it pertained to bishops and deacons *quasi ex officio* is apparent from the Didache (c. 15) and the Apostolic Constitutions.[30] Then, too, the consciousness of the command of Christ to teach all nations as it was handed down by the Apostles had developed a vigorous tradition, especially as they concerned the duties of the episcopal office. However, this duty of catechising was not limited to a class of persons permanently set apart for that purpose, but all orders of the clergy were accustomed to take part in the work. Even laymen were encouraged to teach converts the first elements of religion. Systematic instruction was given by those who had been trained for this purpose. In this regard, it is necessary to point to the catechetical schools. In the year 179, a catechetical school was established at Alexandria by St. Pantaenus, among whose successors are listed Clement of Alexandria (d. 217) and Origen (d. 254). Within a short time similar schools opened at Rome, Antioch, Odessa, Nisibis, Jerusalem and Carthage, where an efficient clergy was trained, and Catholic doctrine was successfully defended against heretical attacks.[31] These schools eventually developed into the cathedral or episcopal schools of the Middle Ages. The second observation to be noted is that the matter of instruction was rather limited. It was necessary that the candidate for Baptism know the Creed and the Lord's Prayer.[32] The major part however was moral in tone as is evident from the Didache, the writings of the Fathers particularly

[29] Reichel, *Complete Manual of Canon Law*, I, 35-50.

[30] *Const. Apostolorum*, VIII, 32—*MPG*, I, 1127.

[31] Joly, *Histoire de la Civilisation*, p. 139; Lalanne, *Influence des Pères de l'Eglise sur l'Education*, p. 19.

[32] Concil. Laodicea (363), Canon 46,—Mansi, II, 571; Synodus Trulla (692), Canon 78,—Hefele, *Hist. of the Councils*, V, p. 233.

of St. Cyril of Jerusalem [33] and St. John Chrysostom [34] and St. Augustine's famous work *De Catechizandis Rudibus*.

From the point of view of legislation, it can be said that custom was the strongest influence in shaping the catechetical instruction given during this first period. Taking its origin in the Apostles, especially from St. Paul, it was developed by the Apostolic Fathers. With the freedom of the Church after the Edict of Milan (313) and the corresponding increased conciliar activity, regulations centered more around the conduct and conditions of the catechumenate, the principal purpose of which was proper and thorough preparation for Baptism.

Section 2. The Sixth Century to the Thirteenth Century

As with the Apostles, so now, after the fall of the Roman Empire in the West, new difficulties presented themselves with the barbarian invasions. With the same zeal the Church set about for her spiritual conquest, in increased missionary activities—St. Augustine in Britain (604), St. Patrick (495) and St. Columban in Ireland (615), St. Boniface in Germany (754/5), St. Ansgar among the Danes (865), St. Adalbert among the Slavic races (997) and St. Stephen in Hungary (1038). The logical consequence was careful vigilance in the proper instruction of the people. In this regard, a complete change in ecclesiastical discipline concerning catechesis evolves. Contributing factors were the decline of the catechumenate due to the difficulties involved in adult instruction protracted over such a long period of time; and the growth of the practice of infant Baptism.[35] Therefore, while in the first period, the emphasis was instruction as preparatory to Baptism, from this time on it is provided after the reception of this sacrament.

In this period also the legislation of the Church in the West is exclusively considered. The growth and rapid spread of Islamism through the East and northern Africa, together with the schismatical

[33] Catechetical Lectures—Nicene and Post-Nicene Fathers (Second series), VIII, 4.

[34] *Catechesis ad illuminandos*—*MPG,* XLIX, 223.

[35] Göbl, *Geschichte der Katechese im Abendlande vom Verfalle des Katechumenats bis zum Ende des Mittelalters,* p. 1.

separation begun under Photius crushed the growth of Christianity in those parts of the Empire. As a consequence, therefore, whatever legislation was enacted would scarcely be of any import.

Article 1. Obligation of Bishops and Priests [36]

In the early part of the Middle Ages now under consideration, bishops went from place to place working as catechists. In addition, they had to see that Christianity was kept alive, once it had been established in a community. This was accomplished principally by sermons, so that at first, there is not a clear distinction between sermons and catechetics, but rather the sermons themselves were catechetical. The second Council of Braga in Portugal (572) describes the obligation of bishops as providing both for the proper instruction of their priests relative to the administration of Baptism and the people themselves.[37] That the bishops were particularly zealous in the fulfillment of their obligations is more evident from their activity than from express legislation. St. Boniface, in the Council of Leipzig (743), admonishes his priests to teach the Apostles' Creed and the Lord's Prayer to their flocks so that they will know them from memory. Furthermore he provided that renunciation and confes-

[36] Since legislative provision for instruction divides itself into three channels the obligation of bishops and priests, that of parents, and that of sponsors—it is more convenient to trace its indications in this manner, rather than by territories.

[37] Canon 1: "Placuit omnibus episcopis, atque convenit, ut per singulas ecclesias episcopi per dioeceses ambulantes, primum discutiant clericos, quomodo ordinem baptismi teneant, vel missarum: et qualiter quaecumque officia in ecclesia peragant. Et si recte quidem invenerint, Deo gratias agant: si autem minime, docere debent ignaros, et hoc modis omnibus praecipere, ut sicut antiqui canones jubent, ante viginti dies baptismi, ad purgationem exorcismi catechumeni currant: in quibus viginti diebus omnino catechumeni symbolum, quod est, 'Credo in Deum Patrem omnipotentem,' specialiter doceantur. Postquam ergo in his suos clericos discusserint, vel docuerint episcopi, alia die, convocata plebe ipsius ecclesiae, doceant illos, ut errores fugiant idolorum, vel diversa crimina: id est, homicidium, adulterium, perjurium, falsum testimonium, et reliqua peccata mortifera; aut quod nolunt sibi fieri, non faciant alteri: et ut credant resurrectionem omnium hominum, et diem judicii; in quo unusquisque secundum sua opera recepturus est. Et sic postea episcopus de ecclesia illa profiscatur ad aliam."—Harduin, III, 386.

sion of faith which takes place at Baptism, should be given in the vernacular language.[38] Theodulph of Orleans (797), in a circular letter, admonishes his clergy to give earnest instruction to the people, at least the Creed and the well-known instructions in faith and morals.[39] Bishop Jesse of Amiens in a pastoral letter gives a good insight into the religious instructions of the early part of the Middle Ages: every pastor should not only himself have all the faith necessary, but through the living word, he should also teach those who are under him the truths of faith. For this reason, it is his duty to know all his parishioners, men, women, and children, and the condition of their life. Moreover he is to teach each one the Lord's Prayer and the Creed; from time to time he should also have them recite these for him.[40] The Synod of Liege (710) reminds priests [41] to explain carefully the moral law and those elements of faith which are necessary for salvation. The *Regula Canonicorum* of Bishop Chrodegang (762) of Metz calls attention to the obligation of pastors to instruct the youth of their parishes.[42] Furthermore the second Council of Clovesho (747) in England provided that priests should not only instruct their people concerning the Creed and the Lord's Prayer, but also teach them the prayers for Mass, for Baptism, and the ceremonies which are observed in the administration of the

[38] Statuta, XXV: "Annuntient etiam presbyteri omnibus fidelibus sibi subjectis Symbolum et Orationem Dominicam memoriae commendare . . ."—Hartzheim, I, 74. Statuta, XXVII: "Nullus sit presbyter qui in ipsa lingua qua nati sunt, baptizandos abrenuntiationes vel confessiones aperte interrogare non studeat, ut intelligant quibus abrenuntiant."—Hartzheim, I, 74; *MPL*, LXXXIX, 822. It was due to the influence of St. Boniface that the vernacular language was introduced in the Germanic territory as the medium of instruction. Hezard, *Histoire du Catéchisme*, p. 107.

[39] Göbl, *Gesch. der Katechese*, p. 77.

[40] Göbl, *op. cit.*, p. 79.

[41] Canon 4: "Diligenter eis explicet praecepta Dei; et diebus Dominicis exponat ea quae ad salutem sunt animarum."—Hartzheim, I, 32.

[42] Caput 48: "Solerter Rectores Ecclesiarum vigilare oportet, ut pueri et adolescentes qui in congregatione sibi commissa nutriuntur, vel erudiuntur, ita jugibus Ecclesiasticis disciplinis constringantur; ut eorum lasciva aetas, et ad peccandum valde proclivis, nullum possit reperire locum, quo in peccati facinus proruat."—Hartzheim, I, 110.

Sacraments. It further provided that this was to be done in the language of the country.[43] The Council of Chelsea (787) repeated practically the same obligations.[44]

Further stimulus for the provision of adequate instruction was given at the beginning of the Empire, the influence of Charlemagne (787-802) being especially noteworthy. The general aim was for a well-trained clergy [45] in order that they in turn could competently fulfill their obligations to their people. Synodal decrees and pastoral letters of bishops constantly reminded priests of their duty. Typical is the letter of Ghaerbaldus, Bishop of Liege, both in showing the influence of the emperor and in outlining the care and diligence with which they should educate their people.[46] Among the outstanding figures of the ninth century can be mentioned Riculfe of Soissons, Herard of Tours, Vulfade of Rheims, Raoul of Bourges; and in the

[43] Canon 11—Harduin, III, 1955. Like Boniface in Germany, the Venerable Bede (735) was particularly influential in having the vulgar tongue introduced as the medium of instruction in England. *Cf.* Hezard, *Histoire du Catéchisme,* p. 111.

[44] Canon 2—Harduin, III, 2073.

[45] In 787, Charlemagne issued to all the bishops and abbots the Capitulary, *Epistola de Litteris Colendis,* the exemplar of which was sent to Baugulf Abbot of Fulda. Its purpose was to renew among the clergy and religious a love of study, that they might become fitting instructors. *MPL,* XCVIII, 896.

[46] "Cognoscatis, quia Epistola Domni et Serenissimi Imperatoris nostri ad nos venit, quae relicta in praesentiam nostram, ubi comperimus, quia domnus noster (Carolus magnus) existimat, nostram esse negligentiam, ut non adnunciemus populum pleniter de oratione Dominica, ut sciant, et symbolum, quod Apostoli docuerunt: et Domno nostro dictum est, quia nostra pigritia sit, qui Sacerdotes sumus in populo, et praedicare et docere populum debemus, qualiter per rectam fidem, et orationem, et opus bonum, ad coelestia regna perveniant; et ex ea parte credo, quod vestra aliquorum negligentia sit: propterea mandamus vobis, atque contestamur per tremendam omnipotentis Majestatem, ut negligentes de hac re amplius non existatis, sed pleniter cum omni studio, et omni diligentia, ut unusquisque vestrum ad suam basilicam vel in quantascumque basilicas missarum solemnia celebrat, praedicare et commonere unusquisque juxta modum capacitatis suae faciat de praecepto Dei omnipotentis, et verbo Domni nostri Imperatoris sui, et parvitatis nostrae, quia tantum pondus nobis suprapositum inter vos partire debemus, ut unusquisque orationem Dominicam, id est, 'Pater noster, qui es in coelis,' et reliqua, quae sequuntur, et Symbolum, sicut docuerunt Sancti Apostoli, discere, et in memoria retinere studeat, et ore proferre . . ."—Hartzheim, I, 359.

tenth century Burchard of Worms, Yves of Chartres and Bonizo of Sutri.[47]

The Synod of Aix la Chapelle (802) provided that priests should teach not only the meaning of the Creed and Lord's Prayer, but also the complete meaning of a Christian life; it was further provided that the people themselves were to be examined concerning their knowledge of the Lord's Prayer and the Creed, in order to determine whether or not they understood these correctly, and whether they knew them from memory.[48] Again the Council of Aix la Chapelle (836), demanded that the priest give the faithful every opportunity to learn the Our Father, the Creed, how to live a Christian life, and how to better themselves if they had fallen into sin.[49] The Council of Paris (829),[50] the Council of Mayence (847), under Rabanus Maurus, Abbot of Fulda,[51] and the Council of Tribur (895) [52] repeated the same obligations, namely, of instructing the faithful in the Lord's Prayer, the Apostles' Creed, the virtues and vices in the vernacular language so that they would be able to understand these. In the *Libellus de Ecclesiasticis Disciplinis* written toward the end of the ninth century, the obligation of priests to instruct their parishioners in the Creed and the Lord's Prayer was imposed.[53] Pope Eugene II, at the Council of Rome (826) demanded of the clergy to teach all to protect and nourish the faith which they vowed in Baptism; that they should not neglect to learn and know from memory the Lord's Prayer and the Creed in order that every one would confess orally that which he believed in his heart, and in accordance with the vows of Baptism; and that they should keep the commandments, with sincere charity for God and neighbor.[54]

[47] Hezard, *Histoire du Catéchisme*, pp. 134, 135.

[48] Synodus et conventus exeunte anno 802 Aquisgrani habita. Capitula a sacerdotibus proposita, V; capitula de examinandis ecclesiasticis, VIII and IX—*MGH, Capitularia Regum Francorum*, tom. I, 106, 107.

[49] Canon 2—Hartzheim, I, 289.

[50] Canon 6—Harduin, IV, 1300; Canon 3 (Sixth Council of Arles, Mansi, XIV, 59).

[51] Cap. 2—Hartzheim, II, 154.

[52] *De Praedicatione Presbyterorum*—Hartzheim, II, 409.

[53] Canon 272 (from the Council of Rheims)—Hartzheim, II, 481.

[54] Canon 3—Mansi, XIV, 1003.

Article 2. Obligation of Parents

With the downfall of the catechumenate, it was left principally to the parents themselves to provide for the proper religious training and education of their children.[55] The personal fulfillment of this natural obligation was more necessary both because of the unorganized condition of the Church and because of the number of Christians living in outlying rural districts where the assistance of the clergy was meager.[56] Therefore, the Church frequently reminded the parents of their obligation towards their children. Chrodegang, Bishop of Metz (760) made it a rule that older and higher classes of people should be taught first that they could instruct the youth.[57] So too the sixth Council of Arles (813) imposed on parents the duty of instructing their children.[58] The Council of Mayence (813) speaks in rather severe terms concerning the necessity of this obligation, providing that those who were neglectful should be punished in some way.[59] Bishop Jonas of Orleans (825) in the letter *De Institutione Laicali* indicated how highly important is the parental obligation of instruction in the home.[60] The *Libellus de Ecclesiasticis Disciplinis* (899) repeated the same obligation.[61] A further indication of the manner in which this duty was held is found in the confessional formularies of this period, where one of the points pertains to the duties of parents in this regard.[62]

[55] Hinschius, *System des Katholischen Kirchenrechts,* IV, 477.

[56] Göbl, *Gesch. der Katechese,* p. 19.

[57] Regula Canonicorum, Canon 83—Hartzheim, I, 182.

[58] Canon 19: "Ut parentes filios suos erudire summopere studeant, quia eos genuerunt et eis a Domino dati sunt."—Harduin, IV, 1006.

[59] Canon 45: "Symbolum, quod est signaculum fidei, et orationem dominicam discere semper admoneant sacerdotes populum Christianum. Volumusque ut disciplinam condignam habeant qui haec discere negligunt, sive in jejunio, sive in alia castigatione emendentur. Propterea dignum est, ut filios suos donent ad scholam sive ad monasteria, sive foras presbyteris, ut fidem catholicam recte discant, et orationem dominicam, ut domi alios edocere valeant. Et qui aliter non potuerit, vel in sua lingua hoc discat."—Mansi, XIV, 74.

[60] Göbl, *Gesch. der Katechese,* p. 22.

[61] Canon 274—Hartzheim, II, 482.

[62] Göbl, *Gesch. der Katechese.* An interesting piece of evidence relative to the duties of parents is from an original document of the twelfth century: *Unde ein jeglich wirt in sinem hûse lêre in* (*den Glauben*) *sîniu chint unde sine*

Article 3. Obligation of Sponsors

The use of sponsors at Baptism takes its origin during the period of the catechumenate where it was their duty to help in the administration of the sacrament. With the introduction of the practice of infant Baptism, however, the sponsor became the representative of the child, with the corresponding duty to instruct the child in the faith which he has professed in the name of the baptized. Instances of this concept of the purpose of sponsors are found in the Councils of Clovesho (747) [63] and Chelsea (787). The Council of Arles [64] in the year 813 declared the same obligation in as much as they are as tutors to the child. The *Libellus de Ecclesiasticis Disciplinis* [65] emphasized the same.

Article 4. Summary

The legislative provisions for catechesis during the first half of the Middle Ages has three characteristics that are conspicuous. The first is the meagerness of the material for instruction—the Creed and the Lord's Prayer constituting the principal part, with some reference to the moral law. While it is true that the obligations of bishops and priests included a more detailed instruction, it must be kept in mind that the parents and sponsors exercised the greatest influence, which accounts for this meagerness. Secondly, the importance of educating the youth by the clergy was not emphasized.[66] Finally, the position of Charlemagne as the outstanding figure of influence manifests itself in a twofold manner. In the first place, by his capitularies and epistles which influenced the bishops to greater vigilance; and secondly, by the establishment of schools. He founded his own palatine school under the direction of Alcuin, the renowned scholastic of York, that it might be a model throughout the empire.[67]

undertân, i.e., "and let every master in his house teach it (the Faith) to his child and to those under him." Göbl, *Gesch. der Katechese*, p. 25 in nota.

[63] Canon 11—Harduin, III, 1955; Canon 2—Harduin, III, 2073.

[64] Canon 19—Harduin, IV, 1006.

[65] Canon 273: "Praecipimus ut unusquisque compater et proximi spirituales suos Catholice instruant."—Hartzheim, II, 482.

[66] Hinschius, *System des Kathol. Kirchenrechts*, IV, 477, 478.

[67] West, *Alcuin and the Rise of Christian Schools*, p. 45.

To Alcuin in turn is attributed the first catechism which takes the form of question and answer. This work was entitled *Disputatio puerorum per interrogationes et responsiones.*[68] Worthy of mention, also, is his thirty-third epistle addressed to Charlemagne in which he outlines the subject-matter that should be learned as preparatory to Baptism, including a knowledge of the last things, the mystery of the Trinity and Incarnation.[69] That such a thorough instruction was given to a very limited number is evident.

The political, social and religious crises which followed in the tenth and eleventh centuries ended legislative enactments respecting catechetics, with efforts rather towards reforming the moral and intellectual condition of the clergy.[70]

Section 3. Thirteenth Century to the Council of Trent

As the Church emerged from the trials of the Iron Age, several factors once more reënkindled her important missionary office. Among these must be enumerated, first of all, the energizing influence of the truly great Pontiffs, such as Gregory VII (1073-1085), Alexander III (1159-1181), Innocent III (1198-1216) and Gregory IX (1227-1241). Secondly, the specter of heresy once more forced the Church to lay weight on the fulfillment of the office of teaching and preaching. History testifies to their ever-present existence from this century with Arnold of Brescia, the Cathari, and the Albigensian sect, to the present-day errors. In truth this fact has constantly proved to be a real stimulus to vigilance on the part of the Church,

[68] Hezard, *Histoire du Catéchisme*, p. 117.

[69] " . . . igitur ille ordo, in docendo verum aetate perfectum diligenter, ut arbitro, servandus est, quem beatus Augustinus ordinavit in libro cui *De Catechizandis Rudibus* titulum praenotavit. Prius instruendus est homo de animae immortalitate, et de vita futura, et de retributione bonorum malorumque, et de aeternitate utriusque sortis. Postea pro quibus peccatis et sceleribus poenas cum diabolo patiatur aeternas; et pro quibus bonis vel benefactis gloria cum Christo fruatur sempiterna. Deinde, fides Sanctae Trinitatis diligentissime docenda est, et adventus pro saluti humani generis Filii Dei Domini nostri Jesu Christi in hunc mundum exponendus, et de mysterio passionis illius, et veritate resurrectionis et gloria ascensionis in coelos, et futura ejus adventu . . . et hac fide roboratum, homo et praeparatus baptizandus est."—*MPL,* C, 190.

[70] Göbl, *Gesch. der Katechese,* p. 86.

reflected not only in her activity, but in her legislation as well. Another important influence was the clarification of doctrine brought about by scholars and theologians in the newly formed universities of the time, which could not help but make itself felt also on the mind of the people. Finally, but of no less importance, must be mentioned the regulation of the fourth Council of the Lateran (1215) which imposed the obligation of confessing and receiving Holy Communion once a year. This made adequate instruction imperative, especially for the youth.[71]

Article 1. Decretum of Gratian

Of the Corpus Juris Canonici, the Decretum alone refers to the obligaton of instruction. It must be pointed out, however, that two canons refer to the catechumenate which no longer existed in the twelfth century.[72] Nevertheless, Canon 57 [73] of the fourth Distinction refers to the obligàtion of the priests in instructing those about to be baptized. In defining the obligation of bishops, the Decretum (C 12, C. X, q. 1) repeats the first Canon of the second Council of Braga (572), which provided that bishops were to instruct both priests and people.[74]

The nature of the Decretum as such, that is, a collection of previous legislation, explains these citations. If an evaluation is to be

[71] Hinschius, *System des Kathol. Kirchenrechts*, IV, 478.

[72] "Ante baptismum, catechizandi debet hominem prevenire officium ut fidei primum catecuminus accipiat rudimentum. Prius ipse Christus ceci nati oculos luto ex sputo facto superlinivit, et sic ad aquas Syloe misit, qui prius debet baptizandus fide incarnationis Christi instrui, et sic ad baptismum iam credulus admitti, ut sciat, cujus gratiae in eo particeps, et cui iam deitor fiat deinceps." C. 54, D. IV, *de Cons.* This canon is taken from Rhabanus, *De Institutione Clericorum*, lib. I, c. 25

"Ante viginti dies baptismi ad purgationem exorcismi catecumini currant, in quibus viginti diebus omnino symbolum quod est: 'Credo in Deum Patrem Omnipotentem' spiritualiter doceantur." C. 55, D. IV, *de Cons.*—from the second Council of Braga (572), Canon 1.

[73] "Catechismi baptizandorum a sacerdotibus uniuscujusque ecclesiae possunt fieri, sicut in sancta hac Romana ecclesia (cui Deo auctore, ministerium nostri famulatus exhibemus) solemniter fieri comprobantur."—C. 57, D. IV, *de Cons.* —from a letter of Pope Nicholas I (858-867) to John, Archbishop of Ravenna.

[74] *Cf.* 12 supra.

made, it seems that some importance is to be attributed to the fact that it preserves the terminology of *catechismus* as referring to instruction. However it is again necessary to turn to conciliar legislation for the legal provisions for instruction.

Article 2. France

The Synod of Utrecht (1294) carefully outlined the obligations of priests, requiring that on each Sunday they were to explain in the vernacular the Creed and the Lord's Prayer; and that once a month or at least three or four times during the year they were to explain the commandments and the seven sacraments.[75] The same was repeated in the Council of Utrecht (1310).[76] The Synod of Albi (1254), in order to strengthen Christians in their Faith and to protect them against the errors of the Albigensian heresy, obligated pastors on all Sundays and feast days to explain the articles of Faith to the people; it also warns parents to bring their children above seven years of age to instruction.[77] The Council of Lavour (1386) was even more detailed and emphatic in outlining instruction to be given on Sundays and feast days, under threat of excommunication for failure to do so, in the articles of Faith, the commandments, the seven capital sins, and whatever else is necessary to be known.[78] The Synod of Tournay (1481) enjoined on pastors the obligation of

[75] Canon 11: "Item praecipimus districte in virtute sanctae obedientiae rectoribus et presbyteris universis et singulis, ut in eorum parochiis, Pater noster, et Credo, praeter articulos fidei qualibet Dominica nec non decem praecepta, et septem sacramenta Ecclesiae semel in mense, vel saltem ter aut quater in anno populo intelligibiliter et lingua materna exponant."—Hartzheim, IV, 22.

[76] Canon 9—Hartzheim, IV, 169.

[77] Canons 17 and 18—Mansi, XXIII, 836, 837; Hefele, *Conciliengeschichte*, VI, 721.

[78] Canon 1: " . . . Ut igitur tam perniciosae ignorantiae et in rectoribus et in subditis occuramus, et per nos ac per fratres nostros suffraganeos parari valeat deinceps Domino plebs perfecta, atque in nostrarum provinciarum civitatibus et dioecesibus doctrina vigeat salutaris: in primis hujus praesentis concilii auctoritate statuimus, et nihilo minus sub poena excommunicationis praecipimus, quatenus universi et singuli rectores ecclesiarum in aliqua provinciarum nostrarum consistentium, diebus Dominicis et festivis in suam parochiam ex more ad Divina conveniant, ipsos parochianos suos et subditos, sicut opportunum fuerit, et secundum gratiam ac sufficientiam unicuique a Domino datam, de ipsius fidei nostrae principiis sive articulis, de decem praeceptis Divinae legis,

instructing the faithful and the children especially in the articles of Faith in preparation for the worthy reception of the sacrament of Confirmation.[79]

Article 3. England and Ireland

A council held in Dublin in 1186 (*Concilium Hibernicum*) reminded pastors of their duty to instruct the youth. It was given in rebuke of the excesses of the time.[80] The Council of Durham (1217-1226) reminded priests to teach their subjects in the right Faith; and imposed on the archdeacons the task of preparing a written explanation of the articles of Faith for the priests in simple words in order that, according to this, they could teach their subjects in the mother-tongue; the same prescription is also found in the *Concilium Scoticum* (1225).[81] The Synod of Lambeth (1281) under Archbishop John Peckham of Canterbury, gave one of the most complete outlines of the obligation of pastors thus far. Every three months the pastor himself, or through his representatives, should hold catechetical instructions for the people in a simple manner; this could also be held on one or more Sundays or holydays following each other. The subject matter of these instructions was to include the fourteen articles of Faith, the ten commandments, the two evangelical precepts of charity, the seven capital sins, and the sins that come under them, the seven virtues, and the seven sacraments. In addition, the synod itself outlined a short explanation of these listed points in order that no cleric could excuse himself because of ignorance.[82]

de septem peccatis mortalibus, et si qua sunt alia quorum sit cognitio necessaria ad salutem, non simul quidem de omnibus, sed alternatim et seorsum prout tempus et locus et capacitas auditorum exigent, diligenter instruant et informent . . . "—Mansi, XXVI, 485; Hefele, *Conciliengesch.*, VI, 721.

[79] Canon 6—Hartzheim V, 526 and 531. In addition, there must be noted an important medium of instruction in the work of the famous Chancellor of the University of Paris, Gerson (1363-1429) entitled *L'Ouvrage de trois parties*. Briefly, the first part contains an explanation of the articles of Faith and the precepts; the second, the manner of confessing properly; and the third, prayers for the dying. This work was used extensively throughout France. *Cf.* Hezard, *Histoire du Catéchisme*, pp. 156-158.

[80] Mansi, XXII, 525.

[81] Mansi, XXII, 1223—Canon 3.

[82] Cap. 9—Mansi, XXIV, 410.

Article 4. Spain

The synodal constitutions of Valencia (1255) obligated pastors to the careful instruction of the faithful, and particularly of the children.[83] The Council of Vallodolid (1322) instructed pastors that on Christmas, Easter, Pentecost, the Assumption of the Blessed Virgin, and the Sundays of Lent they were to explain to the people the commandments, the sacraments, the articles of Faith, and the virtues and vices.[84] The Council of Tortosa (1429) designated as a matter of instruction, the articles of Faith, the Lord's Prayer, the ten commandments, and the seven capital sins; it further provided that learned and capable men were to prepare a book of instruction for this purpose, which was to be conveniently divided into six or seven lessons in order that the contents could be preached on Sundays throughout the year.[85] The Council of Aranda (1473) punished pastors with a fine who did not have the articles of Faith, the Lord's Prayer, the commandments and sacraments written in order that they might preach concerning these from Septuagesima to Passion Sunday inclusive.[86]

Article 5. Germany

Particularly in the last century before the Council of Trent were the commands for instruction repeated frequently in the particular councils of Germany. The Council of Strasbourg (1435) prescribed that on Sundays during Mass when the priest spoke to the people, he was to explain the symbolum in the vernacular.[87] The Council of

[83] Mansi, XXV, 354.

[84] Cap. 2: "Quia notitia catholicae fidei cuilibet orthodoxo est necessaria ad salutem, et ejus ignorantia periculosa quam plurimum et nocivia: statuimus, ut quilibet rector parochialis ecclesiae in scriptis habeat in Latina et vulgari lingua articulos fidei, praecepta decalogi, sacramenta ecclesiae, species vitiorum et virtutum, et quater in anno ipsa publicet populo, in festis videlicet Nativitatis Domini, Resurrectionis, Pentecostes, et in Assumptione Virginis gloriosae, et in diebus Dominicis Quadragesimae. Quod si rectores in hoc negligentes fuerint, per praelatum suum acriter puniantur."—Mansi, XXV, 698.

[85] Canon 6—Mansi, XXVIII, 1118.

[86] Canon 2—Mansi, XXXII, 385.

[87] Canon 56—Hartzheim, V, 245.

Eichstadt (1447)[88] the provincial Council of Salsburg (1454),[89] the Synod of Passau (1470),[90] the Synod of Worms (1497),[91] provided for careful instruction by those having care of souls of both the youth and adults.

Article 6. Summary

The legislative enactments of the various countries in the latter half of the Middle Ages without a doubt produce a striking contrast to those which preceded them. Perhaps the most outstanding feature is that the subject matter of instruction is enlarged as well as more clearly defined. Furthermore, the particular legislation of the various countries provided for the instruction of the people in the vernacular tongue. Written outlines were provided by law for the first time. Due to the better organized parochial system, the weight of the obligation was placed more on the pastors, than on the parents and sponsors, in contrast to the first half of the period under consideration. Finally, the appointment of a definite time of instruction on Sundays and feast days is defined by law more consistently.

In concluding this period before the Council of Trent, it only remains to point out that throughout these first sixteen centuries of the Church's mission to teach all men, there was no legislation of universal import.[92] This furnishes the opening note in the consideration of the final period previous to the Code.

Section 4. The Sixteenth Century to the Code

Many problems confronted the Church as the storm of the Protestant revolt broke over the Christian world. These essentially concerned the faith and its preservation, and a well-educated people therefore was necessary for their proper solution. The Council of Trent (1545-1563) laid the foundation by a clear definition of the doctrines of the Church and by distinct regulations for the instruction of the people. The latter have been the basis of all legislation

[88] *De Praedicatione Verbi Dei*—Hartzheim, V, 364.

[89] *Advisamenta Generalia totam Proviciam respicientia*—Hartzheim, V, 945.

[90] Canon 3—Hartzheim, V, 477.

[91] Canon 34—Hartzheim, V, 665.

[92] Hinschius, *System des Kathol. Kirchenrechts.*, IV, 479.

pertaining to catechesis that has since resulted. Moreover they have been one of the noteworthy influences that has enabled the Church to meet the problems of heresy.

ARTICLE 1. TRIDENTINE REGULATIONS

The canons of the Council of Trent defined the obligations for catechetical instruction in general terms. The preaching of the Gospel of Christ was stated as the principal duty of bishops.[93] Relative to instruction, as distinct from preaching, archpriests and those having the care of souls were commanded to teach the people on Sundays and feast days those things that are necessary for salvation.[94] Furthermore on these days, all priests, both secular and religious, were to teach the children the rudiments of faith and obedience towards God and parents; and, if necessary, they were to be compelled to fulfill this duty under threat of censures.[95] Lastly, the council prescribed the preparation of a catechism of Catholic doctrine:

[93] Sess. V, *de reformatione*, cap. 2: "Quia vero Christianae reipublicae non minus necessaria est praedicatio evangelii quam lectio, et hoc est praecipuum episcoporum munus: statuit et decrevit eadem sancta synodus, omnes episcopos, archiepiscopos, primates et omnes alios ecclesiarum praelatos teneri per se ipsos, si legitime impediti non fuerint, ad praedicandum sanctum Jesu Christi evangelium . . ."

[94] Sess. V, *de ref.*, cap. 2: ". . . Archipresbyteri quoque, plebani, et quicunque parochiales vel alias curam animarum habentes ecclesias quocunque modo obtinent, per se, vel alios idoneos, si legitime impediti fuerint diebus saltem dominicis et festis solemnibus plebes sibi commissas pro sua et earum capacitate pascant salutaribus verbis: *docendo* quare scire omnibus necessarium est ad salutem, annunciandoque eis cum brevitate et facilitate sermonis vitia quae eos declinare et virtutes, quas sectari oporteat, ut poenam aeternam evadere et coelestem gloriam consequi valeant . . . Itaque ubi ab episcopo moniti trium mensium spatio muneri suo defuerint, per censuras ecclesiasticas seu alias ad ipsius episcopi arbitrium cogantur, ita ut etiam, si ei sic expedire visum fuerit, ex beneficiorum fructibus alteri, qui id praestet, honesta aliqua merces persolvatur, donec principalis ipse resipiscens officium impleat."

[95] Sess. XXIV, *de ref.*, cap. 4: "Iidem (episcopi) etiam saltem dominicis et aliis festivis diebus pueros in singulis parochiis fidei rudimenta et obedientiam erga Deum et parentes diligenter ab iis, ad quos spectabit, doceri curabunt, et si opus sit, etiam, per censuras ecclesiasticas compellent, non obstantibus privilegiis et consuetudinibus."

> that the faithful may approach the sacraments with greater reverence and devotion, the holy synod commands all bishops not only to explain, in a manner accommodated to the capacity of the receiver, the nature and use of the sacraments, when they are to be administered by themselves; but also to see that every pastor piously and prudently do the same, in the vernacular language, should it be necessary and convenient. This exposition is to accord with a form to be prescribed by the holy synod for the administration of all the sacraments, in a catechism, which bishops will take care to have translated faithfully into the vernacular language, and expounded to the people by all pastors.[96]

One of the last acts of the council was to provide that this catechism be first approved by the Roman Pontiff.[97]

The composition of this catechism was entrusted to a group of cardinals and theologians, the guiding spirit of which was the saintly cardinal of Milan, Charles Borromeo.[98] Whether it was actually begun before the close of the Council seems doubtful.[99] It was completed, however, in 1564[100] and was published by the authority of St. Pius V in 1566. At the command of the Pontiff, the work was translated into Italian, French, German, and Polish. It was intended

[96] Sess. XXIV, *de ref.*, cap. 7: "Ut fidelis populus ad suscipienda sacramenta maiori cum reverentia atque animi devotione accedat, praecipit sancta synodus episcopis omnibus, ut non solum, cum haec per se ipsos erunt populo administranda, prius illorum vim et usum pro suscipientium captu explicent, sed etiam idem a singulis parochis pie prudenterque, etiam lingua vernacula, si opus sit et commode fieri poterit, servari studeant, juxta formam a sancta synodo in catechesi singulis sacramentis praescribendam, quam episcopi in vulgarem linguam fideliter verti, atque a parochis omnibus populo exponi curabunt; nec non ut inter missarum solemnia aut divinorum celebrationem sacra eloquia et salutis monita eadem vernacula lingua singulis diebus festivis vel solemnibus explanent, eademque in omnium cordibus, postpositis inutilibus quaestionibus, inserere, atque eos in lege Domini erudire studeant."

[97] Sess. XXV, *continuatio sessionis. de indice librorum et catechismo . . .* : "de catechismo a Patribus, quibus illud mandatum fuerat . . . exhibeatur Romano Pontifici et ejus judicio atque auctoritate terminetur et evulgetur."

[98] Scannell, "Doctrine, Christian," *The Catholic Encyclopedia,* V, 75.

[99] Pallavicino, *Istoria del Concilio di Trento,* lib. XXIV, c. 13.

[100] "Catechismum habemus jam absolutum . . ."—Letter of St. Charles Borromeo to Cardinal Hosius, December 27, 1564. *The Catechism of the Council of Trent* (tr. by J. Donovan), 9 in nota.

as a "fixed form of instructing the faithful in the truths of religion from the very rudiments of Christian knowledge; a form to be followed by those to whom are lawfully intrusted the duties of pastor and teacher."[101] The importance of the Tridentine catechism cannot be overemphasized in as much as it became the source of doctrine as well as the basis for the numerous catechisms in simpler form that have since been compiled. Subsequent legislation, instead of describing the subject matter to be taught, prescribed the use of this compendium of Christian doctrine.[102]

The institution of the Confraternity of Christian Doctrine is also identified with the Tridentine period. Its origin is attributed to a certain Milanese, Marco de Sadis Cusani, who organized in Rome, around the year 1562, a unit of zealous men for the proper instruction of children and adults in the doctrines of the faith.[103] By the constitution *Ex Debito* St. Pius V ordered these confraternities to be erected[104] wherever possible in order that instruction would be adequately provided. Paul V (1605-1621) erected the confraternity into an archconfraternity to be established at the basilica of St. Peter's[105] as the center around which the confraternities were to be gathered and directed; he also determined the indulgences and favors for those doing the work of the confraternity.

[101] *Catechismus Tridentinus,* ix.

[102] It is important also to mention the catechism of St. Peter Canisius, S.J. This work, begun by the Jesuit Claudius, was completed by Canisius in 1554, entitled *Summa Doctrina Christiana.* It was published anonymously with a second edition appearing in 1566. A summary, *Institutiones Christianae sive parvus catechismus catholicorum,* by Canisius, appeared in 1561, which was also edited in a simpler form for children under the title *Kleine Katechismus.* Not only in Germany but also in Spain were these catechisms used extensively. Their importance rests in the fact that they counteracted the influence of the catechisms published by Martin Luther. Probst, *Gesch. der Katholischen Katechese,* p. 41.

[103] Fanfani, *De Jure Parochorum,* p. 200 in nota.

[104] ". . . atque tot societates seu confraternitates quot ad hoc tam sanctissimum opus (*i. e.,* of catechizing) exercendum eis opportunae videbuntur, inibi auctoritate nostra erigant, et instituant."—Pius V, const. *Ex Debito,* 6 Oct., 1571 —*Fontes,* n. 141.

[105] Paul V, Breve *Ex Credito Nobis,* 6 Oct., 1607—*Bullarii Romani,* XI, n. LXXXVI.

In summarizing the threefold influence of the Tridentine period —legislation, the catechism, and the confraternity—Monsieur Dupanloup aptly writes: "Hardly had the Church uttered her voice, when on all sides an admirable zeal was shown for the work of the Catechism. A multitude of councils confirmed and published the decree of Trent with a multitude of details which shows the importance they attached to it; men of the highest merit devoted themselves to seeing that the decrees were carried out; and to perpetuate the happy influence of it in the Church, societies were formed solely occupied with the care of giving instructions and Christian education to children." [106]

Article 2. Particular Legislation After the Council of Trent

It was left to the provincial councils to give effectiveness to the Tridentine regulations. This was especially true in regard to catechetical instruction in as much as these councils determined in a particular manner how the general decrees of Trent were to be carried out. Because this particular legislation gives sequence to the historical development of catechesis from a canonical viewpoint, it is necessary to indicate at least what is typical of the efforts of the provincial councils.

The zeal of St. Charles Borromeo is especially manifested in the provincial councils held under his authority. Respecting catechetics, it was provided that instruction was to be given on all Sundays and holydays to the children at a stated hour in the afternoon; at the same time, also, adults were to be instructed in the Lord's Prayer, the angelic salutation, the commandments, the sacraments, and the ceremonies.[107] The second council (1569) commanded bishops to establish the confraternity in the parishes of their dioceses; and a small catechism was to be edited also for its special use. In places where it was impossible to establish these sodalities, two or three laymen were to be selected who were to bring the children to the parish priest for their religious training.[108] In the third council

[106] Dupanloup, *The Ministry of Catechizing*, p. 14.

[107] I Council of Milan, 1565, Canons 4 and 6—Mansi, XXXIVa, 7 and 9.

[108] Canon 2—Mansi, XXXIVa, 108.

(1573) bishops were once more admonished to establish the confraternity in parishes that had neglected to do so. It also obligated regulars, having the care of souls, to give the necessary training in Christian doctrine.[109] Finally in order to make certain that the people were learning the truths necessary for salvation, the fifth Council of Milan (1579) imposed the obligation on all confessors that they should have their penitents recite the Lord's Prayer, the Hail Mary, the Apostles' Creed, and the commandments before beginning their confession. If ignorant, the penitent was not only to be cautioned with regard to the seriousness of this obligation, but also the task of learning these was to be imposed as a penance. In addition, pastors, during Mass or Vespers, were to recite together with the people some of the principal chapters of Christian doctrine, after which one of these was to be thoroughly explained. The Roman Catechism was to be used as a guide. Parents and those having servants were reminded of the importance of their duty to instruct those under their care.[110]

The regulations of the Council of Rome (1725) are noteworthy in their detailed outline of instruction for youths and adults. On the afternoon of each Sunday and holyday, all children between the ages of seven and fourteen were to be taught Christian doctrine for which Bellarmine's catechism was to be used. Moreover the parents were to supplement this instruction not only by word and example, but also by reviewing the catechism together with their children.[111] In

[109] Canon 13—Mansi, XXXIVa, 161.

[110] Const. 2—Mansi, XXXIVa, 347, 348. Similar legislation is to be found in the following provincial councils: Council of Ravenna, 1568, cap. 1—Mansi, XXXVa, 590; I Council of Lima, 1582, cap. 3-9, in which it was provided that instruction be given both to the Spanish and Indians in their separate languages —Mansi, XXVI, 197-199; Council of Bordeaux, 1583, tit. 18 and tit. 20—Mansi, XXIVa, 767 and 769; Council of Rheims, 1585, cap. 1—Mansi, XXIVa, 686; Council of Toulouse, 1590, cap. 3—Mansi, XXIVb, 1277; Council of Avignon, 1594, tit. 42—Mansi, XXIVb, 1355; Council of Aquileia in Illyria, 1596, tit. 4—Mansi, XXIVb, 1379; Council of Tarragona, 1685, const. 2—*Coll. Lac.*, I, 743; Council of Naples, 1699, cap. 3-6—*Coll. Lac.*, I, 159.

[111] Cap. 4: "invigilent etiam Episcopi, ut Parochi propria, quae sua sunt, munera exerceant: . . . hora vero pomeridiana pueros puellasque, a septennio et supra ad annum usque decimumquartum, propriam convocandos in paroeciam curent; eosque suo ordine et loco per Ecclesiam dispositos, maribus semper a

addition the council indicated the method according to which these classes were to be conducted: one or two of the devout students (or clerics) were to pass through the streets with a bell, announcing the hour for class, *O patres et matres, mittite filios vestros ad Doctrinam Christianam alioquin strictam Deo reddituri estis rationem.* Some laymen were appointed to gather and keep them in order. According to age, the children were separated into four groups. The class itself, one hour in length, was to be so arranged that during the first half-hour, an explanation of some topic was given; during the second half-hour, the students were to ask each other questions. The class was concluded by the recitation of the Apostles' Creed, the Lord's Prayer, the Hail Mary, the commandments, the sacraments, and the act of contrition.[112] Adults, on the other hand, were to be instructed each Sunday during the sacrifice of the Mass in order that they would know and understand the principal truths of Catholicism.[113] If pastors were negligent in fulfilling this obligation, they were to be punished with suspension; adults, especially the parents, who disobeyed these precepts, were to be personally interdicted.[114]

Article 3. Benedict XIV (1740-1758) and Clement XIII (1758-1769)

Benedict XIV issued several important enactments which pertained to catechetical instruction. In his encyclical letter *Ubi Primum,* the pontiff addressed the bishops of the Church relative to the duties of their office. Among the most important of these, he

foeminis separatis fidei rudimentis doctrina seu christiana ex libello, quam clar. mem. Cardinalis Bellarminus edidit . . . et quo poterunt, plana imbuant unam semper eademque docendi regulam sequentes." "Puerorum vero parentes adhortari non omittant, quos etiam adhortamur Nos et admonemus, ut proprios filios domi bonis moribus, verbis, et exemplis instituant atque ea, quae ad Christianam doctrinam pertinent, sedulo edoceant, eadem crebro, quae illos Parochi edocuerint, repetentes."—*Coll. Lac.,* I, 347.

112 Appendix: *Instructio ad facilitandam methodum docendae doctrine Christianae.*—*Coll. Lac.,* I, 401, 402.

113 Cap. 5—*Coll. Lac.,* I, 347.

114 Appendix—*Coll. Lac.,* I, 402.

enumerated the necessity of vigilance in seeing that pastors diligently trained their flocks in the truths of religion. Moreover, it was insisted that no contrary custom was to excuse the fulfillment of this pastoral obligation.[115] Negligence on the part of pastors was already in evidence at the time of Innocent XIII (1721-1724) and Benedict XIII (1724-1730). Each of these pontiffs had admonished priests that no contrary custom could remove this important obligation; moreover, that it existed even though schools and the activities of certain parishes lightened the burden.[116]

The most important legislation of this pontiff, however, is contained in the encyclical letter *Etsi minime*. It treated expressly with catechetics, and together with the canons of Trent and the *Acerbo nimis* of Pius X, it forms the basis for the present law of the Code. Its provisions can be summarized thus: (1) The obligation of imparting the knowledge of the truths of faith belongs to the bishop who is to discharge this duty through the pastors. (2) To assist pastors in this work, the bishop is to appoint tonsured clerics and those in major and minor orders. This is a new provision in the universal law of the Church. (3) Parents are to be brought to understand the seriousness of their obligation in seeing that their children are properly educated in the catechism. (4) Approval is given to the assistance of both lay men and women in the work of instructing the children; in addition, the erection of sodalities is recommended. (5) The sacraments of Holy Eucharist and Confirmation are not to be administered to those ignorant of the truths of religion. Likewise parties to marriage must know the essentials of Catholic doctrine. Finally confessors are reminded of the invalidity of absolution given to those who are ignorant of those truths necessary to be known *necessitate medii*. (6) Universal recognition and recommendation is

[115] N. 3: "In id vero potissimum quoque incumbite, ut quicumque animarum curam gerunt, diligenter diebus saltem Dominicis, aliisque festis de praecepto, plebes sibi commissas, pro sua, et earum capacitate, pascant salutaribus verbis, docendo ea quae Christi-fideles ad salutem scire oportet, ac explicando Divinae legis capita, Fideique dogmata et pueros ejusdem Fidei rudimentis imbuendo, quacumque prava in contrarium consuetudine, ubicumque esset, prorsus sublata."—litt. encycl., *Ubi Primum*, 3 Dec., 1740—*Fontes*, 304.

[116] Innocent XIII, const., *Apostolici ministerii*, 23 May, 1723, N. 11—*Fontes*, n. 280; Benedict XIII, const., *In Supremo*, 23 Sept., 1724, N. 3—*Fontes*, n. 283.

given to the catechism of St. Robert Bellarmine in order that the method of teaching and learning Christian doctrine be uniform.[117]

The constitution *Firmandis* defined the right and duty of bishops, in the visitation of parishes conducted by Regulars, to see that proper instruction was given in Christian doctrine both to the children and the adults.[118] And in the encyclical letter *Cum Religiosis* the same pontiff again reminded the bishops of Italy that parties to marriage were to be well instructed. This was occasioned by the fact that many persons, coming to Rome to apply for matrimonial dispensations, were ignorant of the truths of religion.[119]

Clement XIII required that the catechism of the Council of Trent should be used universally throughout the Church. On the occasion of the condemnation as heretical of an Italian version of a French work entitled *Exposition de la Doctrine Chrétienne, ou, Instructions sur les principales vérités de la Religion,* he commanded that this catechism be the norm of faith and discipline. It is important to note the reasons which were given for this decision, namely: that this work contains the doctrine which is common to the Church and is free from all error; and, on the other hand, the use of manuals prepared carelessly would give rise to scandals and contentious controversies because of lack of agreement.[120]

Article 4. Nineteenth Century

The documents relative to catechesis which the pontiffs issued during this period can better be classified as hortatory than as legis-

[117] Benedict XIV, litt. encycl., *Etsi minime,* 7 Feb., 1742—*Fontes,* n. 324. At the request of Pope Clement VIII (1592-1605), Bellarmine compiled two catechisms, the first entitled *Dottrina Cristiana Breve* for children, the second *Dichiarazione piu Copiosa della Dottrina Cristiana* for teachers. These works appeared in 1597. Together with the Catechism of the Council of Trent, they have exerted a profound influence in the accomplishment of the work of catechetics. They have been translated into more than fifty languages.—*De Operibus S. Roberti Bellarmini,* p. 40. Clement VIII ordered that these be used in the city of Rome and surrounding districts by the confraternities of Christian Doctrine.—Breve, *Pastoralis Romani,* 15 July, 1598—*Dichiarazione della Dottrina Cristiana,* p. 3.

[118] Benedict XIV, const., *Firmandis,* 6 Nov., 1744—*Fontes,* n. 349.

[119] Benedict XIV, litt. encycl., *Cum Religiosis,* 28 June, 1754—*Fontes,* n. 429.

[120] Clement XIII, const., *In Dominico agro,* 14 June, 1761—*Bullarii Romani Continuatio,* V, n. CCXXIX, 522-525.

lative. In order to stimulate bishops and pastors to vigilance in the proper education of youth and adults, as well as to warn them against the dangers threatening from the spread of protestantism, communism, and socialism, Pius IX (1846-1878) admonished them to special care in this regard.[121] Leo XIII (1878-1903) in like manner stressed particularly the obligation of parents as arising from the natural and divine law.[122]

In contrast, however, the legislative enactments of provincial councils throughout the Christian world stressed more and more the necessity of a thorough religious training and instruction. In general, they stipulated first, that pastors and parents should be alert to provide for the proper religious instruction of children; secondly, that the prescribed outlines of the teaching method were to be followed; thirdly, that catechism were to be published, based either on the Tridentine catechisms or that of Bellarmine; [123] fourthly, that the *catechism of perseverance* was to be used for those who had made their first communion; and lastly, that the Confraternity of Christian Doctrine, together with the Sunday school classes, were to be established in all parishes.[124]

[121] Pius IX, litt. encycl., *Nostis et Nobiscum*, 8 Dec., 1849—*Fontes*, n. 508; ep. to Card. Rodrigues, Patriarch of Lisbon, *Quo graviora*, 8 July, 1862—*Fontes*, n. 535.

[122] "E qui fin dal principio, in virtu del Nostro pastorali ministero, Ci e d'uopo tornare alla mente di ogni cattolico il dovere gravissimo, che per legge naturale e divina gl'incombe d'istruire la sua prole nelle sopranaturali verità della fede." Leo XIII, ep., *in Mezzo,* 26 June, 1878—*Fontes*, n. 574. "Hoc igitur parentes reputent, se magnum quidem onus gerere de liberorum tuitione, multo tamen gerere majus, ut eos ad meliorem potioremque vitam quae animorum est, educant.," ep. *Officio Sanctissimo*, 22 Dec., 1887—*Fontes*, n. 596.

[123] For a detailed list of the number of catechisms published in the various dioceses of France up to this time, *cf.* Hezard, *Histoire du Catechisme*, 275-472.

[124] Council of Paris, 1849, cap. 4—*Coll. Lac.*, IV, 22; Council of Avignon, 1849, tit. 1, cap. 7—*Coll. Lac.*, IV, 326; Council of Turin, 1849, dec. xv—*Coll. Lac.*, IV, 272; Council of Toulouse, 1850, tit. iv., cap. 3—*Coll. Lac.*, IV, 1065; Council of Albi, 1850, tit. II, dec. 7—*Coll. Lac.*, IV, 414; Council of Bourges, 1850, tit. vi, decr. "de catechizandis pueris,"—*Coll. Lac.*, IV, 1129; Council of Lyons, 1850, dec. 15—*Coll. Lac.*, IV, 476; Council of Sens, 1850, tit. iv, cap. 3—*Coll. Lac.*, IV, 902; Council of Bordeaux, 1850, tit. I, cap. 5—*Coll. Lac.*, IV, 555; Council of Orange, 1851, tit. iv, cap. 6—*Coll. Lac.*, IV, 1204; Council of Vienna, 1858, tit. iv, cap. 4—*Coll. Lac.*, V, 181; Council of Cologne, 1860 and 1863, tit. II, cap. 22, and tit. II, cap. 4—*Coll. Lac.*, 365 and 637; Council of Prague, 1860,

In the United States, the hierarchy found it necessary, for the preservation and spread of the faith in their constantly growing dioceses to make legislative enactments with regard to the teaching of catechism. Of special importance are the provisions of the councils of Baltimore, some of which still exert an influence on present-day catechetical activity. The first diocesan synod of Baltimore (1791) under Archbishop Carroll ruled that in parishes where there were more than one priest, instruction was to be given to the children and laity on each Sunday afternoon; in parishes with only one priest, this instruction was to be given after Mass.[125] The first provincial council (1829) recalled the obligations of the Tridentine decrees; moreover, it provided for a new catechism to be edited according to that of Bellarmine.[126]

In the first plenary council (1852) the bishops of Charleston, Buffalo, and St. Louis were appointed to compile a catechism in English, and the bishop of Philadelphia to compile one in German, which were to be adopted for use throughout the country upon the approval of the Holy See.[127] The council repeated the obligation of pastors to provide for the proper instruction on Sundays and holydays of obligation.[128]

The second plenary council (1866) gave more detailed regulations for the religious training of youth. In addition to its command to build schools wherever possible, it provided further, that parents themselves were to instruct their children; also, that four times each year, especially around the ember days, pastors, for a period of several days, were to prepare those who had not as yet made their first communion. Seven years was determined as the age for the reception of the sacrament of Penance; and if, at that age, the child could

tit. II, cap. 6—*Coll. Lac.*, V., 449; Council of Utrecht, 1865, tit. II, cap. 6—*Coll. Lac.*, V, 809; II and III Councils of Tuam in Ireland, 1855 and 1858, dec. 17 and dec. 8—*Coll. Lac.*, III, 862 and 877; I and II Councils of Quebec, 1851 and 1854, dec. 11 and dec. 15—*Coll. Lac.*, 614 and 653.

125 Sess. V—*Concilia Provincialia Baltimori Habita*, 20, 21.

126 Decreta 29 and 33—*op. cit.*, 82, 83.

127 Congregatio quinta privata—*Concilium plenarium Baltimori Habitum*, 29-31.

128 Decretum 12—*op. cit.*, 46, 47.

realize the Real Presence of Christ in the Blessed Sacrament, he was to be admitted to Holy Communion.[129]

The third plenary council (1884), while retaining the above decrees, again reminded pastors to care assiduously for the proper instruction of the youth; it was emphatic in declaring this to be the proper duty of the pastor and to be fulfilled by himself as far as possible. It determined that those about to make their first Holy Communion were to be taught three times each week for a period of six weeks; and after first communion, this instruction was to continue for two years. Finally, the council made provision for the preparation of a new catechism, both because of the inadequacy as well as the lack of uniformity in the several catechisms then in use.[130]

Article 5. Pius X (1903-1914)

The final legislation of a universal character, previous to the Code, which dealt with catechetics, is contained in the encyclical letter *Acerbo nimis* of Pius X. It reaffirmed the provisions of the *Etsi minime,* and in addition, prescribed the following regulations to be enforced in every diocese throughout the Christian world: [131]

(1) Parish priests and those having the care of souls, on each Sunday and feast day throughout the year, were to teach both boys and girls those things they must believe and do to be saved, and that

[129] Tit. IX, cap. I—*Concilii Plenarii Baltimorensis II. Acta et Decreta,* 222-225.

[130] Tit. VII, cap. II—*Acta et Decreta Concilii Plenarii Baltimorensis Tertii,* 118, 119.

"One of the most interesting, albeit perplexing, pages of American Catholic history lies beneath the enactments on the catechism. The desire for a uniform catechism was never absent from the thoughts of our spiritual leaders from the days of John Carroll." Guilday, *A Short History of the Councils of Baltimore,* p. 239. Before the appearance of the catechism of Baltimore in 1885, the most popular work was Challoner's "Abridgement of Christian Doctrine" (1772). Others included those of Father Molyneaux (1785), Butler (1788), Morechals (1818), England (1821) and Flaget (1825)—*op. cit.,* 239, 240.

[131] N. 17: "Haec Nos quidem Venerabiles Fratres, auctoritate apostolica constituimus et jubemus. Vestrum modo esset efficere ut, in vestra cujusque dioecesi, nulla mora atque integre executioni mandentur . . ." Pius X, litt. encycl., *Acerbo nimis,* 15 April, 1905—*Fontes,* n. 666.

this instruction be given as far as possible with the aid of the catechism.

(2) At stated times during the year, they were to prepare boys and girls to receive the sacraments of Penance and Confirmation by continued instruction over a period of several days.

(3) Every day during Lent and, if necessary, on other days after Easter, they were, by suitable instruction and reflections, to prepare boys and girls to receive their first Holy Communion.

(4) In each parish the Confraternity of Christian Doctrine was to be canonically instituted. Through this organization, parish priests, especially in places where there was a scarcity of priests, were to find valuable helpers for catechetical instruction in pious lay persons whose duty it was to lend their aid to this holy and salutary work, both from zeal for the glory of God and as a means of gaining the numerous indulgences granted by the Sovereign Pontiffs.

(5) In large towns, and especially in those where there were universities, colleges, and grammar schools, religion classes were to be organized in order that those young people, attending these schools, could be instructed in the truths of faith and in the practice of Christian principles.

(6) In consideration of the fact that adults, no less than the young, stood in need of religious instruction all parish priests and others having the care of souls, were to explain the catechism to the faithful on all days of obligation. This was to be done in an easy style suited to the intelligence of their hearers. This instruction was to be given at such a time of the day as would be deemed most convenient for the people, but was not to conflict with the hour when the children were taught. In this instruction the catechism of the Council of Trent was to be used as a guide. The subject matter was to be so divided that within a space of four or five years, the entire catechism would be explained.[132]

In order to complete these regulations, Pius X also reformed the Constitutions of the Archconfraternity and confraternities of Christian Doctrine which had been laid down by Paul V. He established a congregation, with the vicar-general of Rome as president, to govern the archconfraternity; and under whose jurisdiction, the confrater-

[132] N. 16—*Fontes,* 666.

nities were to be organized. In regard to the latter, it stipulated that a decree of the ordinary of the place was necessary for their canonical erection, which decree, together with a petition for confirmation, had to be sent to this congregation.[133] Finally, in order that the importance of the pastoral obligation would be emphasized, negligence in giving the commanded instructions was specified as a just cause for removal from a parish.[134]

By these enactments, the legislation respecting catechetics was given a definite and universal form. What had been generally expressed by Benedict XIV was given specific determination, especially in regard to the time and manner of instructing the children. They met present-day conditions in a twofold manner, namely, by providing for the instruction of those attending public schools, and by re-emphasizing the need for the continued instruction of adults in order that they might have an intelligent understanding of the dogmas of the Church. As such they furnish the foundation for a major portion of the present legislation of the Code.

Article 6. Conclusion

It remains only to indicate the principal features of the development of catechesis from the canonical viewpoint. As is evident, the legislation of the first period had but little effect on subsequent legislation. It concerned itself with the regulation of the catechumenate, and with the passing of the latter, these laws fell into desuetude. The one contribution, however, were the sponsors at baptism, whose duty relative to the instruction of their spiritual children, was determined in the legislation of the subsequent periods. The steady expansion of the Church in the West, following the fall of the Roman Empire, resulted in anxious solicitude for the religious training of the people. As a consequence, therefore, the duties of bishops and priests, as well as parents and sponsors, was repeatedly defined. These obligations were determined more specifically as the external organization of the Church became more firmly knit together. The canons of the Coun-

[133] Pius X, Breve, *In Litteris Nostris—ASS,* XXXIX, 35-39.

[134] S. C. Consist. decr., *Maxima cura,* 20 Aug., 1910, no. 8: "Neglectio officiorum parochialium post unam et alteram monitionem perseverans et in re gravis momenti, ut . . . in catechesmi."—*Fontes,* n. 2074.

cil of Trent gave direction to the entire Church in the fulfillment of her teaching mission. As a result, there is a constant mutual relationship between particular and the universal legislation respecting religious instruction, the former determining more accurately, according to the varying conditions of each country, the specifications of the latter.

CHAPTER III

THE OBLIGATION OF LOCAL ORDINARIES

ARTICLE 1. THE NATURE OF THEIR OBLIGATION

Canon 1327, § 1: Munus fidei catholicae praedicandae commissum praecipue est . . . Episcopis pro suis dioecesibus.

§ 2. Episcopi tenentur officio praedicandi per se ipsi Evangelium, nisi legitimo prohibeantur impedimento; et insuper, praeter parochos, debent alios quoque viros idoneos in auxilium assumere ad huiusmodi praedicationis munus salubriter exsequendum.

The immediate source of this canon is the mandate given by Jesus Christ to the rulers of His Church to "teach all nations," [1] "to preach the gospel to every creature." [2] In thus restating the divine law, the canon specifies those in whom the teaching office of the Church has been vested and in a general way indicates the manner in which they are to discharge their duty.

It is evident therefore that canon 1327 is fundamental to the canonical legislation which treats with the preaching of the Gospel.[3] For this reason, the word *praedicatio* is not to be understood in its more general meaning as referring to any explanation, either public or private, of Christian truths, such as might be given even by a layman, but in a strict sense as referring to the ministry which our Lord committed to the Apostles and their successors. As such it defines the object of the teaching ministry, namely, the promulgation of the truths contained in the Sacred Scripture and Tradition that men must accept and adhere to in order to attain eternal salvation.[4]

[1] Matt. xxviii. 18, 19.

[2] Mark xvi. 18.

[3] CIC, Lib. III, Pars. IV, Tit. XX.

[4] Blat, *Commentarium Textus Codicis Canonici,* III, 247.

Thus, it may be stated that this ministry, almost by its very nature, embraces three distinct fields of activity, namely, catechetical instruction whose purpose it is not only to teach the rudimentary truths of Christian doctrine to children and others not yet acquainted with them, but also to continue this teaching by a fuller explanation and more complete analysis of the entire field of Christian doctrine, in keeping always with the intellectual ability of those who are being taught; sacred eloquence, distinguished from the former especially by the manner of presentation of the subject-matter, which both supplements instruction and fosters an ever deeper interest in the Gospel teaching; and missions, which on still another plane, assist and inspire men to lead devout lives in accordance with the principles thus learned. It is to be concluded therefore that canon 1327 is basic to the legislation which is concerned with catechetical instruction, and as a consequence of this relationship, the nature of the obligation of local ordinaries to provide for such instruction is determined.

The principal incumbents in providing that the laws which regulate catechetical instruction are properly obeyed are the bishops of the Church under the authority of the Roman Pontiff. The reasons for this are that they are the successors of the Apostles [5] and by divine institution rule over the dioceses committed to their care.[6] To them especially are the words of our Lord addressed: "As the Father hath sent me, I also send you." [7] More accurately, however, does the Code specify that the residential bishops, who are the ordinary and immediate pastors of the dioceses entrusted to them,[8] are bound to fulfill this obligation.[9] Apostolic prefects and apostolic vicars, although lacking episcopal character, are likewise obliged by ecclesiastical law to discharge the same duties.[10]

This obligation as it pertains to local ordinaries is a personal one, not in the sense that they must actually perform this work everywhere

[5] Canon 329, § 1.

[6] Conc. Trid., sess., XXIII, *de sacr. ord.*, c. 4; Bouix, *De Episcopis*, p. 81.

[7] John xx. 21.

[8] Canon 334, § 1.

[9] Canon 336, § 2.

[10] Canons 294, § 1; 301, § 2; *cf.* also Canons 315, § 1, and 323, § 1, which define respectively the obligations of apostolic administrators and abbots and prelates *nullius*.

throughout their dioceses (for this is impossible), but rather that they are personally charged with the responsibility of seeing to it that this ministry is effectively carried out. The reason for this personal responsibility of the local ordinaries is that they are *par excellence* the pastors of their dioceses and the divinely constituted judges in matters of faith and morals. Moreover, they have been chosen because of personal qualifications to break the spiritual bread for their flocks.[11] It would seem that they are only bound to the actual work of catechizing in their place of residence.[12] As a consequence therefore this duty is not to be delegated unless they are legitimately impeded from fulfilling it. Among such impediments are to be enumerated sickness, absence, diocesan visitation, attendance at councils or synods, hostile invasions, extensive diocese, and the like.[13]

As indicated by the canon, pastors and other capable persons are to be appointed to perform the work of catechizing in the various parishes. The reference to *viros idoneos* seems to include only priests in this instance because the canon is treating with the ministry of preaching which is proper to the clerical state; it insinuates moreover that the men chosen must have those particular qualifications which belong to the clergy, namely, sufficient familiarity with the Sacred Sciences, and the necessary moral virtues that are so essential together with those natural gifts which facilitate the accomplishment of this work.[14] The ordinaries are thus free to call upon any member of the diocesan clergy to assist in the various activities of the catechetical program. In addition, they may request religious superiors, either of exempt or non-exempt houses in their dioceses, to supply assistants wherever they might be needed. Seminarians and members of the laity may be employed in a similar manner. A more complete discussion of this phase is reserved however to succeeding pages.

While the force of the word *salubriter* is to be emphasized when considered in its relation to the preaching ministry, yet it seems to have a slightly different connotation according as it is applied to

[11] Augustine, *A Commentary on the New Code of Canon Law*, VI, 340.

[12] S. C. P. F., Nov. 28, 1785—Coll. S. C. P. F. (ed. 1907), n. 581.

[13] C. 15, X, *de. off. jud. ord.*, I, 31.

[14] Augustine, *Commentary*, VI, 340.

catechetical instruction and to preaching (*concio* and *missio*). In general, however, it may be said to indicate that the minister is to explain the Gospel of Christ in a sound manner, so that the people will have an intelligent grasp of the truths necessary to be assented to, the virtues to be practiced, and the dispositions necessary to gain eternal happiness. In a negative sense it excludes the display of eloquence for eloquence' sake, as well as motives of vainglory.[15]

Therefore it may be stated summarily that local ordinaries, both by divine and ecclesiastical law, have been constituted as official teachers of the Church to announce the truths of the Catholic Faith to the people committed to their care. In pursuance of their duty, they are required to be vigilant lest error should creep in. The fundamental obligation in the discharge of this office is to provide for catechetical instruction.[16]

Canon 1329: Proprium ac gravissimum officium, pastorum praesertim animarum, est catecheticam populi christiani institutionem curare.

This canon specifically defines the duty of giving religious instruction to the Christian people. The notion of catechetical instruction itself demonstrates why it is one of the most important of the pastoral obligations. For the entire Christian structure is of little avail unless the fundamental religious truths and moral principles have been planted deeply in the minds of the Christian people in an orderly manner. Because it is the gravest obligation of pastors of souls, it follows that it must occupy the foremost place in the pastorate. Nowhere does the Code speak more emphatically of the gravity of a duty.[17] While it is defined as an obligation proper to the pastoral office, it is not such in a strictly personal sense. This is evident from the fact that any effective explanation of religious and moral truths must be oral, methodical, and more or less confined to small groups. Likewise it demands a great deal of time. There-

[15] Canon 1347, § 2; Benedict XV, litt. encycl., *Humani generis,* June 15, 1917—*AAS,* IX (1917), 305.

[16] Wernz-Vidal, *Jus Canonicum,* II, 632.

[17] Canon 18.

fore, if it were a strict personal duty, it would be impossible to provide for this instruction in a thorough manner. The word *praesertim* indicates that others besides the pastor of souls are obligated to engage in this work.

Among the pastors, the residential bishops, as *Ordinarii loci,* are especially obligated by reason of their office. They are to provide that the "purity of faith and morals is preserved both amongst the clergy and the laity, that Christian doctrine is taught to the faithful, especially to children and those who are ignorant of the truths of faith." [18] They are to supervise the entire catechetical movement in the diocese committed to their care.

Article 2. Extent of the Legislative Power of the Ordinary

Canon 1336: Ordinarii loci est omnia in sua dioecesi edicere quae ad populum in christiana doctrina instituendum spectent; . . .

This canon defines in a general way that the local ordinaries are to establish the norms which are to regulate religious instruction in their dioceses. This may be done either in the diocesan synod or independent thereof. In both instances, however, the ordinary is not able to prohibit anything that is certainly and expressly commanded or permitted by the Code; for instance, no law could be enacted whereby those who had made their first Communion would be exempt from further instruction; neither is he able to permit anything which is forbidden by the common law.[19] Rather it may be said that the legislative efforts will be directed to determining more accurately the prescriptions of the common law according to conditions as they exist in each particular diocese.

Because of the importance of catechetical instruction as affording the foundation for the entire Christian life, both temporal and eternal, there can be little question but that the force of canon 1336 is

[18] Canon 336, § 2.

[19] Canon 6, § 1; Vermeersch-Creusen, *Epitome,* I, 271; Wernz-Vidal, *Jus Canonicum,* II, 631.

mandatory for the local ordinary. This becomes all the more certain when viewed in relation to canon 335 § 1, which defines not only the right but also the duty of residential bishops to govern the dioceses committed to their care both in spiritual and temporal matters by the exercise of legislative, judicial, and coercive powers. In a certain sense also the phrase *Ordinarii loci est* as used in canon 1336 is restrictive. That is to say, the proper and thorough conduct of the diocesan catechetical program belongs to the local ordinary as the one ultimately responsible for its effective execution. To illustrate this more clearly, school superintendents for example may not define the teaching methods to be used in Christian doctrine classes independently of the local ordinary unless he in turn has permitted them to do so; neither may pastors in the same way select the textbook of Christian doctrine to be employed in the parish classes but rather they must use the one selected by the ordinary. This seems sufficiently clear from the decree *Provido sane* [20] which states:

> Ordinarius quisque perpendat in Domino quid providendum, quid praescribendum supersit pro opere hoc sanctissimo et maxime necessario, quove pacto id quod vult facilius consequi et efficere possit . . .

The same decree likewise provides for the establishment of a diocesan catechetical office as the medium for carrying out efficiently the diocesan regulations. These regulations will include provision for (a) the appointment of capable teachers, (b) the subject-matter of instruction, (c) teaching methods to be employed, and (d) the time and place for giving instructions.[21]

(a) The Appointment of Capable Teachers

A distinction must here be made between those who teach in a public capacity and those who do so privately. In the former class are to be enumerated pastors and other priests. In order that their capability be determined, however, canon 1328 defines that anyone assuming the ministry of preaching (which includes that of cate-

[20] *AAS,* XXVII (1935), 148.

[21] Prümmer, *Manuale Juris Canonici,* p. 472; Vermeersch, *Epitome,* II, 411; Coronata, *Institutiones Juris Canonici,* II, 252.

chizing) must have first received the faculty to do so. It is granted to pastors in virtue of their office, and to other priests by delegation. This faculty, which is called the *missio canonica,* may be defined as the positive deputation, given by the proper ecclesiastical authority to teach Christian doctrine. In order to receive this deputation, the candidate's aptitude must be proved either by an examination or by other means as determined by the ordinary.[22] The necessity of the *missio canonica,* which empowers the recipient to teach *ex officio* arises from the nature of the teaching office as such, in as much as it is not to be exercised until one has been admitted into the body, so to speak, of authorized teachers.[23] In other words teaching in a public capacity implies the right to do so which right must be obtained from the lawful authority who in this instance is the bishop of the diocese.

As indicated above, the law [24] also permits other clerics, religious, both lay and clerical, and laymen and women to be employed by the pastor to assist in the work of religious instruction. This assistance may be either in the capacity of teachers in the schools or as catechists in the parish classes. As is evident, these do not need the deputation of the ordinary in the sense of the *missio canonica* since their position is that of private persons teaching in a private capacity. However, the ordinary may prescribe that they pass an examination and receive his approbation before engaging in this work. In fact it would seem, both from the mandatory character of canon 1336 and from the recent decrees of the Holy See,[25] that such

[22] In his encyclical letter *Humani generis,* Benedict XV has indicated the qualities that should be present in the candidate for this faculty. The first, as is evident, is that he be well instructed in the truths which he is to teach. In addition, he should be so given to the Divine Will that no obstacle will be too great to prevent the accomplishment of this task. Finally, he should be imbued with the spirit of prayer. As the Pontiff wisely counsels: "It is through this spirit of prayer that the salvation of souls is obtained, and not by speaking eloquently or in a subtle manner."—*AAS,* IX (1917), 305.

[23] Conc. Trid., sess. XXIII, *de sacr. ordinis,* Canon 7; Wernz, *Jus Decretalium,* III, 21-23.

[24] Canons 1333 and 1334.

[25] S. C. de Rel., instr., Nov. 25, 1929—*AAS,* XXII (1930), 28-29; *Periodica,* XIX (1930), 199-206; S. C. C., decr., *Provido sane,* Jan. 12, 1935—*AAS,* XXVII (1935), 148.

approbation is necessary. In addition to the power granted to pastors of parishes to engage the assistance of catechists, both clerical and lay, the local ordinaries likewise are to supply suitable teachers as far as is possible for those parishes where they are needed.[26] Because of this, the ordinary may have his seminary students assist in this work, especially during their summer vacation.

(b) The Subject-Matter of Instruction

Apart from any consideration of those to be instructed, the content of Christian doctrine in general may be classified into the following groups: (1) Apologetics, which examines the principal truths concerning man, God, natural religion, supernatural religion, the divinity of Christ and His religion, and the Church. (2) The dogmatic truths as contained in the Apostles' Creed and the definitions of the Church which includes a study of the unity and trinity of God, the mystery of the Incarnation, the position of the Blessed Virgin, the public life of Christ and His death and resurrection, the activity of the Holy Ghost, the Church and its distinguishing marks, the primacy and infallibility of the Pope, the episcopacy, the remission of sin, the resurrection of the dead, the communion of saints, particular judgment at death, purgatory, the general judgment at the end of the world, hell, heaven, and life eternal. (3) Morality, under which is grouped the consideration of the commandments of God and the Church, sin and its species, the cardinal virtues, the evangelical beatitudes, the works of mercy, the states of life, and daily pious exercises of a good Christian. (4) The Sacraments, which includes a study of the nature and kinds of grace together with an examination of each of the seven Sacraments. (5) Liturgy, which will explain the various kinds of prayer, the external solemnity associated with the public acts of worship, especially the Sacrifice of the Mass. (6) History which will include Old Testament History, New Testament History, and a brief review of Church History.[27]

The body of the faithful to which this subject-matter must be explained is divided into three general groups from a canonical point

[26] S. C. C., decr., *Provido sane,—AAS,* XXVII (1935), 149; *cf. etiam,* p. 43.

[27] *Periodica,* XIX (1930), 202-206.

of view, namely, candidates for first Communion, generally at the age of seven, the youth between the ages of seven and fourteen, and adults.[28] From a pedagogical point of view, as is generally agreed upon in the United States, the classification includes youth to the age of seven, seven to thirteen, thirteen to seventeen, college students, and adults. Since this is a problem of teaching, it would seem that the latter is to be adopted. In schools this will present no difficulty. In parish classes, however, the ordinary will need to take into consideration various local conditions in determining the division that is to be followed.

For the instruction of youth, the most important item, however, is to adapt the subject-matter of religious instruction to the mental ability of the various groups. Prescinding from the work of the teacher, this is done chiefly by the proper selection of textbooks of Christian doctrine.[29] Following the opinion previously given, it seems that it is necessary for the local ordinary to approve those texts which are to be used exclusively in the diocese not only for parish classes but also for schools and colleges.[30] In other words, the choice of textbooks does not belong to the pastor or teachers. In addition to the apparent canonical obligation, desire for uniformity in the catechism, at least for those printed in the same language, has been

[28] Canons 1330-1332.

[29] "Textbooks" is used advisedly in this instance in contra-distinction to "catechism," which is commonly accepted to designate question and answer texts. This latter need not of necessity be used, especially for all the groups where teaching methods might best be served by another form.

[30] In order to give the dioceses of the United States a uniform text of Christian doctrine, an episcopal commission was appointed at the meeting of the Hierarchy of the United States in November, 1935, to make a study of the Baltimore Catechism. Under the commission's supervision, schemata for corrections were sent to all the bishops, leading educators and theologians of the country from the National Office of the Confraternity of Christian Doctrine under whose administration the work is being done. When reports were received, they were given to a committee of priests who, after considerable study, submitted a revised text to the committee meeting for the study of the Baltimore Catechism at the National Catechetical Congress held in New York in October, 1936. At the conclusion of the discussion, the proposed revision was put in the hands of the episcopal commission for further study. The text, in question and answer form, is devised for students not below the fifth grade.

frequently expressed by the Roman Pontiffs and many provincial councils, and was a subject of discussion in the Vatican Council.[31] It seems proper, therefore, to list the reasons why such uniformity is important, if not for an entire nation speaking the same language, at least for the province or for the diocese. Because of the fluctuation of the population, not only from country to country, but also within the country itself, confusion in textbooks often leaves the impression that one is studying an entirely new set of doctrinal truths; as a result, there arises confusion of ideas in the minds of the people. At the same time, uniformity would be a stabilizing influence among the people, especially since parents would be enabled to teach and examine their children from the same text with which they themselves are familiar. The unity of understanding that would follow from the use of one text would be a powerful instrument in persuading non-Catholics of the excellence of the Catholic teachings. Moreover, errors would be prevented from creeping into the catechism, and purity of doctrine would thus be easily maintained. That this is important is manifest from the fact that in many instances errors have been found in various catechetical texts. At the same time, the methods employed in teaching the catechism would become more stabilized. Finally, another tremendous advantage that such a work would afford is that a secure foundation and source of Catholic literature, especially that of a polemic and apologetic nature, would be given.[32]

For the instruction of adults, the prescription of Pius X in his encyclical letter is recommended by the decree *Provido sane*:

> In consideration of the fact that in these days adults no less than the young stand in need of religious instruction,

[31] Wernz, *Jus Decretalium*, III, 41; Conc. Vatic. (1869-1870)—*Coll. Lac.*, VII, 663-666.

[32] "Il Catechismo Unico,"—*La Civilta Cattolica*, II (Anno 56-1905), 385-401.

In general the qualities that should characterize a text in question and answer form are: (a) that it be theologically correct in its doctrinal part; (2) in the mechanical part, the number of questions should be reduced to a minimum with the emphasis on "reason" questions rather than "leading" questions. These, together with the answers, should be short and precise, with the use of abstract language reduced to a minimum.

> all parish priests and others having the care of souls shall . . . explain the catechism for the faithful. . . . In this instruction they are to make use of the Catechism of the Council of Trent; and they are to divide the matter in such a way as within the space of four or five years to treat of the Apostles' Creed, the Sacraments, the Decalogue, the Lord's Prayer, and the precepts of the Church.[33]

Of importance still in the United States is the question as to whether the Catechism of Christian Doctrine prepared and prescribed by the Third Plenary Council of Baltimore must be used, for the council decreed as follows:

> . . . Hoc catechismo [a coetu Rmorum. Archiepiscoporum approbato] in lucem edito quamprimum uti teneantur omnes animarum curam habentes, et praeceptores tam religiosi quam laici.[34]

This catechism, when edited, was approved by Archbishop Gibbons in 1885, as is indicated in the text itself: "The Catechism ordered by the Third Plenary Council of Baltimore, having been diligently compiled and examined, is hereby approved," [35] followed by "James Gibbons, Archbishop of Baltimore, Apostolic Delegate." [36] However, there is no evidence to show that this catechism was approved by the archbishops as a body, which the council had expressly stipulated, and as a consequence the approbation of Cardinal Gibbons would not suffice for such a general approbation.[37] Consequently the use of this catechism cannot be said to be obligatory, and therefore the ordinary of the diocese is free to determine the textbook of Christian doctrine to be employed. Likewise, it seems that custom has nullified the force of this decree. For, since 1885, other catechetical texts have been used throughout the various dioceses of the United States, which have had either the express or tacit approval of the ordinaries. The conclusion is obvious, when it is considered that a

[33] N. 6—*Fontes,* n. 666.

[34] *Conc. Plen. Balt. III,* n. 219.

[35] Concerning the discussion relative to the authorship of the catechism, the reader may refer to the *American Ecclesiastical Review,* vols. LXXXI (1929), 573-586; LXXXII (1930), 610-615; XCIII (1935), 613, 614.

[36] *Catechism of Christian Doctrine* . . . on title page.

[37] *HPR.,* XXXIII (1933), 1198-99.

custom of forty years' continuous duration against an ecclesiastical law abolishes this law, provided the custom itself is reasonable and is not expressly reprobated.[38]

(c) *The Teaching Methods*

Religious instruction, just as any other, avails little unless the subject-matter is presented to the student in an orderly manner. This is accomplished by that teaching method especially whose principal aim is to adapt the content of instruction to the mental ability of the various classes. In order to provide that only the most effective methods [39] are used, the Code has wisely entrusted their approbation and recommendation to the ordinaries.

[38] Canon 27.

[39] Among the better known and generally accepted methods of teaching Christian doctrine, are to be listed:

(a) *The Munich Method* (also called the Psychological or Stieglitz method) whose basis is the psychological law that learning proceeds from sensible cognition to the intellectual grasp of the thing as perceived by the senses. Because three phases are distinguishable in learning, namely, impression of the sensory organs, understanding, and conviction, the method in general is divided into three corresponding categories of presentation, explanation, and application. In the first of these, the appeal is to the senses by demonstrating things themselves as far as possible. In explanation, the inductive process is used to arrive at the answer of a question as given in the catechism. Then only is the text of the catechism used in order that the answer be thoroughly memorized. To convince, the method intends all units of study to be centered around our Lord, with emphasis especially on those truths that are of importance in a sincere Christian life.

(b) *The Sulpician Method* [This method owes its origin to Father Jean Jacques Olier (1608-1657)]. The predominant aim of this method is not simply to instruct the children in the truths of religion, but to inspire them to live according to these truths. To accomplish this, the conduct of the catechism class comprises recitation with question and answer, instruction both on the succeeding lesson and the Gospel, and hymns. In addition, this method emphasizes prayer, admonitions, and motivation by prizes, contests, religious processions and other ceremonies on certain appointed days.

(c) *The Sower Method* (this method derives its name from the educational journal, *The Sower,* published quarterly at St. Bede's College, Manchester). This method, in order to avoid the routine memorizing of the catechism, is divided into three steps corresponding to the mental development of the child. The first, in preparation for Holy Communion, emphasizes the play element. The second, which includes children between the ages of eight and twelve, uses the

Because the responsibility of imparting religious instruction belongs particularly to priests, canon 1365, § 3, provides that in their seminary training "there shall also be lectures in pastoral theology, with practical exercises particularly in the manner of teaching catechism to children and others." That it devolves on the ordinary to safeguard the fulfillment of this provision is evident from a letter of the Sacred Congregation of Studies which thus urges the proper training in methods of teaching:

> . . . We earnestly request Your Amplitude to urge strongly this precept of Canon Law and to see to it that in your seminary catechetical training be assiduously cultivated. Let the professor of pastoral theology give frequent instructions on the manner of teaching Christian doctrine; and let the clerics themselves have practical exercises in preparation for this great work, either in the seminary or in churches, as prudence may suggest.[40]

The importance and necessity of effective methods is also explained in the same letter by a quotation from the encyclical *Acerbo nimis* of Pope Pius X:

> It is far easier to find an orator who will speak copiously and beautifully than a catechist whose teaching is in every respect what it should be. Therefore, whatever be the facility in thought and expression with which a person is naturally endowed, let him remember this: He will never treat of Christian doctrine to children or to the people with profit to their souls unless he prepares and makes himself ready by much reflection. They are surely mistaken who, relying on the ignorance or dullness of the people, imagine that they can be negligent in this matter. On the contrary, the more untutored one's hearers are, the more care and dili-

inductive method in arriving at the catechism answers, which are then memorized from the catechism. The final step is introduced when the child has reached the age of twelve. It is one of analysis and criticism in which the appeal is to the child's reasoned judgment. It is practical in scope, looking to the life of the child after he has left school.

For a complete analysis and bibliography of these and other methods, the reader is referred to Bandas, *Catechetical Methods.*

[40] S. C. de Sem. et Stud. Univ., epistola, Sept. 8, 1926—*AAS,* XVIII (1926), 453.

> gence he must use to adapt those sublime truths, in themselves so remote from the common grasp, to the dull minds of the uneducated, to whom they are as necessary as they are to the wise for the attainment of eternal beatitude.

The ordinary may also judge the competence of lay teachers by prescribing certain standards of required knowledge and ability to which they are reasonably expected to conform before receiving his approbation to teach; pastors, in virtue of their training and experience, should watch that the proper methods are observed. In this manner, ample provision is made for the correct and methodical imparting of religious instruction.

(d) Time of Instruction

Both the Council of Trent [41] and the encyclical *Acerbo nimis* [42] laid down the rule that the children be instructed on all Sundays and holydays of obligation. The Code, however, does not mention this, and therefore, according to Canon 6, § 6, this regulation of the old discipline has lapsed.[43] In particular dioceses, however, this law may be reimposed, although the designation of Sundays and holydays is not obligatory.

In the United States, an enactment of the Second Plenary Council of Baltimore [44] relative to teaching children on Sundays and holydays of obligation must be taken into consideration. This question is discussed in the chapter on the obligations of pastors. Suffice it to note here that since this enactment is simply a restatement of the then existing common law, it does not retain its binding force.

It is within the power of the ordinary, although not to the exclusion of the pastor, to determine the time to be devoted in preparing the children for the reception of the sacraments of Penance and Confirmation,[45] and likewise, to provide for the exceptions that might

[41] Conc. Trid., sess. XXIV, *de ref.*, cap. 4.

[42] N. 16—*Fontes*, n. 666.

[43] Fanfani, *De Jure Parochorum*, 197; Cocchi, *Commentarium in Codicem*, lib. III, pars. IV, n. 17.

[44] *Conc. Plen. Balt. II*, n. 128.

[45] Canon 1330, 1°.

arise when instruction for first Communion cannot be given during Lent.[46] Similarly the ordinary must determine by law the length of the catechetical period for the parish classes as well as to define how long, after first Communion, the children are to attend the classes of instruction. Because conditions vary from diocese to diocese, due to circumstances of weather, employment, parochial facilities, and the like, the laws regulating the time to be devoted to religious instruction will be drawn up to meet these conditions.

In some jurisdictions in the United States, it has been provided by statute that children in public schools may be excused for certain periods during the week to attend religious instruction; likewise, the legality of such an arrangement, even apart from statute, has been upheld by a court ruling.[47] Consequently, it will be the duty of the ordinary to prescribe how pastors are to make use of these civil law concessions. This is indicated by the questionnaire attached to the decree *Provido sane*.[48]

Canon 1332 prescribes that the pastor is to instruct adults "on Sundays and holydays of obligation." The question, affecting the power of the ordinary, that immediately arises is whether this canon is to be interpreted as meaning *all* Sundays and feast days throughout the year; or, whether the ordinary can permit that such instruction be omitted for a certain number of Sundays, for example, because of the excessive heat during the summer months? In as much as the canon omits the word *omnibus* as found in pre-Code law,[49] it appears to change rather than give a restatement of the law. Therefore it may be concluded that the local ordinary may allow, for a reasonable cause, the omission of instruction on certain designated Sundays and holydays of obligation. These must be of a limited number, however, as is evident from the canon itself; moreover a further indication of such limitation is had in a response of the S. Congregation of the Council to the question: "Whether the custom of omitting catechetical instruction during the months of October and December to the thirteenth day of January, when men are occupied with farm work,

[46] Canon 1330, 2°.

[47] *Cf.* Supplement II.

[48] *Cf.* p. 59.

[49] Pius X, litt. encycl., *Acerbo nimis*, April 15, 1905, N. 16—*Fontes*, n. 666.

can be upheld?" While the answer was given in the form of a private rescript as interpretative of the pre-Code discipline, it still retains a directive force:

> Idcirco haud est servanda consuetudo intermittendi doctrinam christianam *aliquibus anni mensibus,* licet nemo ad eam huiusmodi temporibus accedat.[50]

(e) The Place of Instruction

On first considering this topic, it would seem that the local ordinary would fulfill the intention of the law by designating the parish church as a suitable place for convening the parish classes. However, since it is desirable that these classes be conducted according to the accepted school methods, the choice of location should be determined by the facility with which a given place will lend itself to the actual teaching process, that is, in its equipment, as for example, desks, blackboards, maps and the like. Therefore, a school is to be preferred, or at least a building that will permit this equipment. Lacking such facilities, it is obvious that the parish church will have to be used. Furthermore, it may be necessary in certain localities where the children live in scattered areas to provide for more than one place of instruction. It is evident that contingencies as they exist in various dioceses will determine the character of the provisions which the local ordinary is obliged to make.

ARTICLE 3. ORGANIZATION OF CATECHETICAL INSTRUCTION

In order to give proper direction to catechetical instruction throughout the dioceses of the universal Church, as well as to provide that the laws of the Code governing the teaching of Christian doctrine are properly observed, His Holiness, Pope Pius XI, by a *motu proprio* of June 29, 1923,[51] established a special office of catechetics

[50] S. C. C., resp. (*in Hortana*), August 8 and 29, 1744—Pallottini, *Doctrina Christiana,* n. 2, *Collectio Resolutionum S. C. Concilii,* VIII, 157.

The similar provision of the Third Council of Baltimore (Tit. VII, cap. 1, n. 214) would cause no difficulty in reference to the same question in as much as the ordinary could dispense in this instance for a good cause, or custom could have removed its binding force.

[51] *AAS,* XV (1923), 327.

within the Sacred Congregation of the Council. In pursuance of its obligations, the Congregation, with the approval of Pope Pius XI, made the following suggestions for the diocesan organization of catechetics, which are to be carried out in each diocese if at all possible.[52] While the decree does not indicate causes that might excuse from such organization, it is difficult to enumerate any which would prevent this. Possibly civil law prohibition could be taken as a norm in estimating the gravity of causes that excuse.

The decree recommends the establishment of a catechetical office in each diocese, which under the personal direction of the ordinary, will serve as the organ by which he will promote, regulate, and direct religious instruction throughout the diocese. The ambit of power entrusted to this office is to include supervision of the teaching of Christian doctrine in all parishes, schools, and colleges, as explained in the preceeding article. The diocesan office, moreover, is to organize courses in religion and catechetical pedagogy to train teachers of Christian doctrine, to examine their ability, and to issue each year a special group of lectures on religion for teachers in both the parochial and public schools in order that they may acquire a deeper and clearer understanding of the subject matter that they are to teach. While these functions are explicitly prescribed for the diocesan office, they are in no way exclusive of others such as the organization and direction of vacation schools, study clubs, and the like. The decree itself, just as the laws of the Code, is wide enough to be accommodated to various conditions as they exist in different dioceses.

In order to consolidate catechetical work, either in an entire country or in an ecclesiastical province, or in the diocese, catechetical congresses are once again recommended according to the decree of the S. Congregation of the Council of the sixteenth of April, 1924.[53] The purpose of these conventions is indicated by the decree itself:

[52] "Praeter haec, ab omnibus servanda, eadem S. Congregatio nonnulla media locorum Ordinariis indigitare opportunum censet, quae, experientia teste, ad optatum finem apta visa sunt, ut eadem vel saltem aliqua in sua quisque dioecesi iidem Ordinarii, pro rerum locorumque adiunctis, adhibenda curent." S. C. C., decr. *Provido sane,* Jan. 12, 1935—*AAS,* XXVII (1935), 150.

[53] S. C. C., decr., April 16, 1924—*AAS,* XVI (1924), 431.

"The immense advantage of having catechetical conventions and other meetings relative to religious instruction, whereby better methods may be learned and promulgated for the more effective and prompt teaching of Christian doctrine to all the faithful, especially to children and young people, is evident to everyone." When such meetings of a provincial or national character are held, the program of the business to be transacted together with the date and place of the meeting *must* be sent to the Congregation of the Council previous to convening. For diocesan conventions, this procedure is not prescribed, but is strongly urged. The reason for this prescription is due to the practice of the Holy See to reserve to itself approval of such actions where the faith and the morals of the people are at stake, and where caution must be taken lest errors creep in, especially in the education of the Christian people in these same doctrines of faith and morals.[54]

According to the decree, *Provido sane,* the ordinary of the place must appoint capable priest-visitors who, each year, shall visit all classes of religion in the diocese. It is their duty to see that the prescriptions of the diocesan organization are carried out in the various parishes, and to report the progress of religious instruction, together with the results and defects to the ordinary. The decree quotes from the encyclical letter *Etsi minime* of Benedict XIV relative to this parochial visitation:

> Plurimum quoque ad christiani populi institutionem conferre poterit, si Visitatores eligantur, quorum alii civitatem, alii diocesim lustrantes, omnia sedulo inquirant, ut certior factus Episcopus, pro meritis cuiusque pastoris, aut praemia decernat, aut poenas.[55]

Finally, in order to stimulate the interest of the people to the necessity as well as to a sincere appreciation of catechetical instruction, there is to be celebrated in each parish the "feast of Christian doctrine" (*festum doctrinae christianae*) on a day to be designated by the ordinary. The solemnities of the feast are to include: (a) a parochial Mass, in which the members of the parish receive Holy

[54] *Periodica,* XIII (1924), 186.
[55] *ASS,* XXVII (1935), 151.

Communion, together with prayers to obtain in greater measure the blessings that flow from religious instruction. There is also to be a special sermon on the necessity of catechetical instruction, in which parents especially are to be admonished to teach their children, and to send them to the parish classes, bearing in mind the divine admonition: "And these words which I command thee this day shall be in thy heart, and thou shalt tell them to thy children." [56] (b) Books, pamphlets, leaflets and other suitable reading matter should be distributed to the people. (c) A special collection is to be taken up for the promotion of catechetical work.

In places where the scarcity of priests makes it impossible for them to teach Christian doctrine, the ordinaries are to do their best in providing suitable *catechists of both sexes* to aid the pastors by teaching catechism in the parochial or public schools and in the remote parts of the parish. Especially those who are enrolled in associations of Catholic Action are to be chosen. At the same time, all Catholic associations and sodalities are urged to interest themselves in this work. The desire of Pope Pius XI as expressed in the *motu proprio, Orbem Catholicum* [57] is again repeated, viz., that under the direction of the bishops, religious societies which are devoted to the work of education should establish classes for the training of lay people who can assist in this work.

Summing up the effects of diocesan organization, the decree states:

> Si haec media et industriae adhibeantur, si huic muneri quo nihil est sanctius, nihil magis necessarium, omnes quibus onus est strenuo constantique animo incumbant, sperandum iure est populum christianum, ab errorum insectationibus sancta et incorrupta doctrina continenter munitum, populum acceptabilem sectatorem bonorum operum exstiturum esse, atque salutares effectus percepturum, quos Romani Pontifices in salutem animarum non semel auspicati sunt.[58]

In conclusion, the decree requests the ordinaries, on their quinquennial visit as prescribed by Canon 340, § 2, to submit a report

[56] Deut. vi. 6.

[57] *AAS,* XV (1923), 327.

[58] *AAS,* XXVII (1935), 152.

to the Sacred Congregation of the Council, on the status of catechetical instruction in their respective dioceses according to the following questionnaire: [59]

I.—For Children

(a) Parish Report

1. How many children are there in each parish, and how many of this number attend catechetical instruction?

2. With what diligence do the pastors fulfill the duty of instrucing the children, and who among these neglect this duty? [60]

Have *scholae paroeciales* (instruction classes) been established in these parishes, with what success, and what methods are employed in teaching Christian doctrine? [61]

4. In what manner do priests and other clerics, who have been appointed to assist pastors in giving instruction, coöperate in this work; who, among these, are negligent or refuse their assistance?

5. Do men and women religious assist the pastor in teaching catechism to the children; who, among these, are negligent or refuse?

6. Has the Confraternity of Christian Doctrine been established

[59] In order that the diocesan office can adequately direct and promote religious instruction in the diocese, it is necessary that it have an accurate knowledge of conditions as they exist in each parish, school, college, and confraternity. This is best obtained by accurate statistics submitted annually from every branch of catechetical activity. The questionnaire can be used as a basis in obtaining this statistical information. It will thus facilitate the preparation of the quinquennial report; and it will point to those activities and places where emphasis is to be placed in the diocesan catechetical program.

[60] This diligence is to be estimated according to the manner by which pastors follow out the norms for instruction and parochial organization as laid down by the diocesan catechetical office.

[61] In referring to the instruction classes as parish schools, the purpose is to indicate that these classes should be given scholastic arrangement as far as is possible. That is, the classes should be divided as the ability of the students demands, that the pedagogical methods employed should be of recognized standard, that the conduct of the classes should be systematic with examinations, marks, disciplinary measures, textbooks, contests, etc. In short, all things ought to concur to give the parochial classes the order and seriousness and atmosphere of a well-conducted school.

in each parish, and how do its members assist the pastor in promoting the work of catechizing?

7. Do other sodalities of lay people, especially Catholic Action Sodalities, aid the pastor in this work?

8. Has a Catechetical Office or an office of a similar nature been established? If not, is it possible to establish such an office?

9. Is the feast of Christian doctrine observed, and how?

10. Have catechetical meetings been held, or other conventions for a similar purpose, and with what success?

11. Has conscientious effort been made to have both parents and children attend the parochial classes? What means have been employed to motivate them to be faithful in their attendance?

12. What impediments hinder the teaching of Christian doctrine; what abuses have arisen, and what means have been or can be employed to eradicate these? [62]

(b) Report of Catholic Schools and Colleges

13. How many Catholic schools and colleges of either sex, especially those recently erected, are there which are under the supervision of the clergy, whether secular or religious, or of Sisters?

14. How many students, whether resident or day-students, are there in each of these schools?

15. How many times during the week are classes in religion held, what methods are employed in teaching, and with what success is religion being taught? [63]

16. How can religious instruction be more efficaciously and usefully employed?

[62] The purpose of this question is not only to detect causes of failure that might arise within the parochial and diocesan organization, but also to ascertain if the right of the Church to fulfill its teaching office is being impeded in any way by the civil authorities.

[63] The repeated insistance on information regarding methods of teaching and their results has as its object to make certain that religion classes, whether, parish, school, or college, are efficiently preparing the students to meet the obstacles which present-day circumstances place in the way of their Faith. Moreover, since constant progress is being made in improving pedagogical methods, their application is important also in the improvement of religious education.

(c) Public School Report

17. Is Christian doctrine taught in any of the public schools and with what success?

18. Is religious instruction, as given in the public schools, subject to the authority and inspection of the Church? If so, how, and in which schools?

19. In which of the public schools is Christian doctrine not taught, and for what reason? How is the religious instruction of the students attending these schools provided for? [64]

20. Are any means being taken, or can any means be employed to secure the teaching of Christian doctrine in the public schools?

II. For Adults

21. Is catechetical instruction provided for adults, aside from the usual sermon on the Sunday Gospel, and when does this instruction take place?

22. With what diligence, and method, and at what time do pastors devote their efforts to the fulfillment of this duty?

23. Do the faithful in each parish attend these instructions, and with what results?

24. What means, accommodated to the circumstances of time and place, are to be judged more suitable to bring about a more profitable religious instruction of adults? [65]

Article 4. Relationship Between the Ordinary and Religious

> **Canon 1336: Ordinarii loci est omnia in sua dioecesi edicere quae ad populum in christiana doctrina instituendum spectent; et etiam religiosi exempti, quoties non exemptos docent, eadem servare tenentur.**

[64] This question indicates that in countries where religious instruction is prohibited in the public schools, provision must nevertheless be made for the religious training of the students who attend these schools.

[65] The decree also provides for parochial organization. This will be outlined in the chapter which deals with the obligation of pastors.

All religious, including those that are exempt, are obligated to observe the diocesan regulations of the ordinary in teaching religion. This will include the prescriptions of textbooks, of method, of time, and of place as they exist in the dioceses where the religious houses are located. From the meaning of the canon, it is clear that both clerical and lay religious institutes are bound to the prescriptions, whether they teach in their own church or in parishes that have been committed to their care or in elementary and high schools and colleges that are conducted by them.[66] However, when exempt religious impart instruction to fellow members of the same institute, they are not obligated to observe the regulations of the local ordinary.

While local superiors are to provide that instruction be given to the members of the religious family,[67] and, moreover, are independent of the local ordinary in this matter, nevertheless the Sacred Congregation of Religious has laid down the following norms to be observed by superiors and superioresses of lay religious institutes: (a) during the time of their probation and the term of their novitiate, young men and women are to review their Christian doctrine and learn it more thoroughly, so that each shall not only know the important religious truths by memory, but shall also be able to explain them correctly; neither shall they be admitted to take their vows

[66] This Canon definitely ends the dispute as to the obligation of regulars to observe diocesan regulations pertaining to religious instruction. It confirms the decisions that had been handed down both by the S. Congregation of Bishops and Regulars, and the S. Congregation of the Council: (a) The former gave this decision: *(Episcopos) posse tamen modum determinare, quo utraque res (doctrinam christianam et catechismum) ab iisdem (Regularibus) peragi queat.* —S. C. Ep. et Reg., March 16, 1866.—*ASS*, II (1866), 157. (b) The following questions were proposed to the S. Congregation of the Council: 1. An Regulares teneantur statutum de quo agitur (catechesis tradenda) in suis ecclesiis ex vi legis synodalis in casu: et quatenus affirmative: II. an cogi ad id possint ab Episcopo uti delegato Sedis Apostolicae in casu: S. Congregatio respondit: in proposito casu servetur mandatum Episcopi. S. C. C., March 2, 1861. *ASS*, II (1866), 186.

[67] Canon 509, § 2, 2°: Curent superiores locales: ut saltem bis in mense, firmo praescripto Canon 565, § 2, christianae catechesis habeatur instructio pro conversis et familiaribus, audientium conditioni accomodata, . . .

Canon 565, § 2: Conversi (*i. e.*, novitii) praeterea, diligenter in christiana doctrina instituantur, speciali collatione ad eos habita semel saltem in hebdomada.

without a sufficient knowledge of these truths as attested by a previous examination; (b) after the completion of the novitiate, all religious who are to engage in teaching Christian doctrine to boys and girls in primary schools, whether public or private, must have a sufficient knowledge both of the catechism and of the accepted catechetical methods of teaching, in order that they shall be able to pass an examination as drawn up by the ordinary of the place or by his appointees for this purpose; (c) if, however, religious men or women are chosen to teach Christian doctrine to boys and girls, not in schools, but in the parish classes, they must procure a testimonial of their qualifications to do so from the diocesan curia.[68]

The first requirement appears to be common to all institutes of lay-religious. It requires that a thorough explanation of the catechism-text be given, the responsibility of which rests with the religious superior. The second refers rather to those religious congregations which are devoted to teaching. While the examination itself is not prescribed, but only the necessary knowledge to pass the same, it does not follow as a consequence that it is left to the option of the local ordinary to provide for such. The reason why the religious in this instance are not obligated to undergo the examination is that the S. Congregation of Religious is not competent to request local ordinaries to give such examinations. The obligation nevertheless would seem to exist from the force of canon 1336. Finally, it is required that a testimonial (diploma) of adequate fitness be obtained from the diocesan curia. While it is possible that in certain instances such diplomas may not be issued (and then there can be no question of an obligation to procure them), the law does not seem to permit this possibility. In addition, it is argued that such diplomas are necessary only when Christian doctrine is taught in religious parishes (*paroeciis religiosis*) because other parishes do not fall within the jurisdiction of the S. Congregation of Religious.[69] However, it seems

[68] S. C. de Rel., instr., Nov. 25, 1929—*AAS*, XXII (1929), 28.

The instruction also provides that the schedule which is used by the Vicariate of Rome may be followed as a norm in drawing up the examination to be passed. This schedule comprises two divisions, the first of which deals with catechetical pedagogy and the second with the subject matter of Christian doctrine. *Periodica*, XIX (1930), 201-206.

[69] *Periodica*, XIX (1930), 200.

to be a question of "who teaches" rather than "where religion is taught"; in other words, the S. Congregation intends that the teaching ability of religious be approved, independent of where they might be sent to exercise this function. In the visitation of these parishes, however, the ordinary may investigate whether the diocesan regulations are observed in teaching adults and children.[70]

> **Canon 1334: Si Ordinarii loci iudicio, religiosorum auxilium ad catecheticam populi institutionem sit necessarium, Superiores religiosi, etiam exempti, ab eodem Ordinario requisiti, tenentur per se vel per suos subditos religiosos, sine tamen regularis disciplinae detrimento, illam populo tradere, praesertim in propriis ecclesiis.**
>
> **Canon 608, § 1: Curent Superiores ut religiosi subditi, a se designati, praesertim in dioecesi in qua degunt, cum a locorum Ordinariis vel parochis eorum ministerium requiritur ad consulendum populi necessitati, tum intra tum extra proprias ecclesias aut oratoria publica, illud salva religiosa disciplina, libenter praestent.**

These canons, which complement each other, indicate that it is the mind of the Church that between the secular clergy and the religious there should be a spirit of mutual coöperation in fostering the religious education of the faithful. Expression has been given to this by the forceful words of Pope Leo XIII:

> The common end (of both) namely the salvation of souls to be effected by the combined efforts, demands this agreement; . . . this is the mark which distinguishes the disciples of Christ . . . [71]

From canon 1334 it is clear that it belongs to the exclusive judgment of the ordinary to determine whether or not the assistance of religious is actually needed. This will depend on conditions as they exist in particular dioceses as, for instance, the lack of secular clergy or lay-teachers, the necessity of having experienced teachers

[70] Canons 615 and 1382.

[71] Const., *Romanos Pontifices,* May 8, 1888—*Fontes,* n. 582.

conduct vacation schools, and the like. As is evident from the context, the ordinary is empowered to seek the assistance of religious, exempt or non-exempt, clerical or lay, and this not only in their own churches or public oratories, but also outside of them. This request is to be made to the proper superior, major or minor as the case may be, who in turn is obliged to fulfill it. While canon 608 does not appear to be strictly preceptive, nevertheless, according to Bondini [72] it contains a true precept which is confirmed by canon 1334.

The fact that exempt religious also are held *per se* to assist in giving religious instruction constitutes a derogation of the privilege of exemption.[73] The canon therefore is to be interpreted strictly. As a consequence the question arises whether exempt religious are bound to instruct youth, since the canon uses the term *populo*. Vermeersch [74] and DeMeester [75] insist that a distinction is to be made between *institutio puerorum* (as used in canons 1330 and 1331) and *institutio populi* (as used in canon 1332) with the result that the question is to be answered negatively. However, they recommend the coöperation of exempt religious as far as is possible. Blat, on the contrary, holds that they are bound to assist in the education of both children and adults upon request by the ordinary.[76] While practically there will be no difficulty, canonically the latter opinion seems rather to be preferred, because the term *populo* in this canon is used generically to include youth also, and therefore admits of no stricter interpretation.

If the discipline of the religious institute will be impaired by fulfilling any request, the superiors are in no way obligated to respect this request. Such would be the case if the work of catechizing was prohibited by the constitution, or if it would be necessary to leave the cloister against the regulations of the same. Likewise if such obligations, as that of choir attendance, or the peculiar work which the institute engages in, such as nursing, cannot be reconciled with teaching; or finally if the common life was to suffer a grave detriment be-

[72] *De Privilegio Exemptionis*, p. 52.

[73] Canons 615 and 618, § 1.

[74] *Epitome*, II, 410, 411.

[75] *Juris canonici et Juris canonico civilis Compendium*, III, n. 1292.

[76] Blat, *Commentarium*, III, 255.

cause the members would be absent for a notable length of time from the religious house.[77]

In order that religious assist in this work, it is necessary that they be designated to do so by their superior, although the ordinary or pastor may request certain ones. However, the religious subject does not have the right to exercise these functions independently of the permission of his religious superior, who may thus obligate his subject in virtue of obedience.[78]

Likewise, the local ordinary, independent of canon 1345,[79] may impose on clerical religious the obligation of giving catechetical instruction on Sundays and holydays at all the public Masses; [80] and when the ordinary commands these instructions to be given in all churches or public oratories, regulars are bound in virtue of canon 1345 to do so even though they were not expressly requested.[81]

A final question that presents itself is whether regulars, apart from any request of the ordinary, need his permission in order to give religious instruction either in their own churches or outside of these. According to pre-Code regulations this permission was not necessary, for neither the constitution *Superna* of Clement X [82] nor the Council of Trent [83] mentions this. The responses of the Congregation of the Council and the Congregation of Bishops and Regulars sustain this opinion.[84] It is also accepted by present-day commentators on the Code.[85]

[77] Vermeersch-Creusen, *Epitome*, II, 410; Augustine, *Commentary*, VI, 348, 349; Coronata, *Institutiones*, II, 257, 258.

[78] Schäfer, *De Religiosis*, p. 570.

[79] Optandum ut in Missis quae, fidelibus adstantibus, diebus festis de praecepto in omnibus ecclesiis vel oratoriis publicis celebrantur, brevis Evangelii aut alicuius partis doctrinae christianae explanatio fiat; quod si loci Ordinarius id praeceperit, opportunis datis instructionibus, hac lege tenentur non solum sacerdotes e clero saeculari, sed etiam religiosi, exempti quoque, in suis ipsorum ecclesiis.

[80] Vermeersch-Creusen, *op. cit.*, II, 411.

[81] Blat, *Commentarium*, III, 593.

[82] June 21, 1670—*Fontes*, n. 246.

[83] Sess. V, *de ref.*, cap. 2.

[84] S. C. C., March 2, 1861—*ASS*, II, 184-189; S. C. Ep. et Reg., March 16, 1866—*ASS*, II (1866), 156, 157.

[85] Coronata, *Institutiones Juris Canonici*, II, 253; Blat, *Commentarium*, III, 257.

Religious superiors are to take care that the celebration of divine services in their own churches (or public oratories) does not interfere with the time appointed for catechetical instruction given in the parochial church. The ordinary of the place is to judge whether any detriment results in this instance.[86]

Article 5. Coercive Powers of the Ordinary

Because the teaching of Christian doctrine to children and adults is so important and essential a duty of the priesthood, the Code has provided for the application of punishments lest abuse, negligence or refusal should render the catechetical regulations inefficacious. The duty of enforcing these regulations, both of the common and particular law, is entrusted to the ordinary of the place in virtue of his jurisdictional power. In its exercise, however, a distinction must be made in accordance with the existence of negligence on the part of pastors, priests and other clerics, religious, or parents.

(a) Removal of Pastors

Canon 2382: Si parochus graviter neglexerit . . . puerorum populique institutionem . . . ab Ordinario coerceatur ad normam can. 2182-2185.

The procedure that is to be followed in punishing pastors is indicated by this canon. Before any thought of its application is considered, however, the ordinary of the place should first admonish the pastor in a paternal manner in order to avoid, if possible, penal

[86] Canon 609, § 3. This norm is given lest the solemnities associated with the celebration of a feast-day should attract people away from the instruction classes. It is practically certain that the Sacrifice of the Mass is not included in those divine offices which might interfere with the catechetical program in the parish church. For the rest, the rule given by Benedict XIV is applicable in determining any detriment or interference: 'In hoc articulo quia certa et communis regula praescribi non potest, id totum relictum esse volumus Prudentiae vigilis Ecclesiae Antistites, qui attenta loci, temporis, personarum, qualitate, expensisque rerum omnium momentis, ita studeat solemnis diei celebritatem cum Doctrina Christiana componere, ne alteri altera sit impedimento." —Benedict. XIV, litt. encycl., *Etsi minime*, Feb. 7, 1742, N. 15—*Fontes*, n. 324.

measures to counteract negligence.[87] If this warning is unheeded, then the ordinary must proceed to punish the pastor, since the word *coerceatur,* as used in the canon, seems to be preceptive.[88] This is not to be done in an arbitrary manner, however, but according to the extra-judicial penal process as defined by Canons 2182-2185:[89]

> Parochum qui officia paroecialia de quibus in can. . . . 1330-1332 graviter neglexerit, Episcopus moneat, in memoriam eius revocans et strictam obligationem qua eius conscientia oneratur et poenas in haec delicta iure statutas.

Every pastor is charged with the responsibility of providing religious instruction for (a) the youth of his parish in preparation for the reception of the sacraments of Penance and Confirmation; and to prepare them in a particular manner for their first Holy Communion; [90] (b) those who have made their first Communion,[91] and (c) adults.[92] These constitute distinct obligations, so that grave negligence to perform any one is punishable according to this process.[93]

To determine the gravity of the negligence is a more difficult task. In order that a canonical punishment be inflicted, there must be a *delictum,* that is, the imputable violation of a sanctioned law which constitutes a mortal sin.[94] In regard to catechetical regulations, how-

[87] Canon 2214, § 2; Suarez, *De Remotione Parochorum,* p. 182.

[88] Coronata, *Institutiones,* IV, 90.

The necessity of thus enforcing catechetical regulations is indicated also in the decree *Provido sane*: "Ordinarius quisque perpendat in Domino quid providendum, quid praescribendum supersit pro opere hoc sanctissimo et maxime necessario, quove pacto id quod vult facilius consequi et efficere possit, animadversurus, si casus ferat, in negligentes vel renuentes poenis ecclesiasticis ad normam canonum 1333, § 2; 2182; . . ."

[89] Lib. IV, Pars III, Tit. XXXII—*De modo procedendi contra parochum in adimplendis paroecialibus officiis negligentem.*

[90] Canon 1330.

[91] Canon 1331.

[92] Canon 1332.

[93] Noval, *De Processibus,* Pars. III, 577-581; Coronata, *Institutiones,* III, 548.

[94] Canon 2195.

ever, it is not necessary that scandal or actual injury to the youth and adults will have resulted from their violation, because these are founded rather on a *praesumptio damni.*[95] To estimate the gravity of negligence, therefore, it is necessary to use the norms established by moral theologians. Among these, the common opinion seems to be that the omission of instruction for a period of three months in the year, whether continuous or at intervals, would constitute a mortal sin.[96] In addition, the norms established by diocesan law, the circumstances of the parish, together with the legitimate customs that exist in it relative to classes in religion, the location of the parish (for example, whether it is a mission parish, a rural parish, and the like), and the spiritual injury which results to the members of the parish, must also be inspected in estimating the gravity of the negligence. The only general rule that can be given is that the gravity is to be estimated according to the prudent judgment of the ordinary, who must take into consideration the norms just mentioned, and in addition, the negligence must be habitual in order to presuppose carelessness and remissness.[97]

In a given case, it is necessary also for the ordinary [98] to have moral certainty that a pastor has failed in his duty. To determine the certainty therefore of this criminal negligence (which may be neither notorious nor altogether certain), a special inquiry must be made into the case, knowledge of which may have come to the ordinary through rumor or denunciation.[99] The manner of performing this inquisition is left to the prudent judgment of the ordinary. Commentators are unanimous in pointing out that no action should

[95] Canon 21; Noval, *op. cit.,* Pars. III, 589.

[96] Vermeersch-Creusen, *Epitome,* III, 176; DeMeester, *Juris Canonici,* II, 312.

[97] Muniz, *Procedimientos Eclesiasticos,* I, 658; Coronata, *Institutiones,* IV, 626; Noval, *De Processibus,* Pars. III, 581; Suarez, *De Remotione Parochorum,* p. 182.

[98] Canons 2182 and 2183 use the word *Episcopus* while the two following use *Ordinarius.* Because of Canon 2382, however, not only bishops but all ordinaries as defined by Canon 198, § 1, may act in this process—Coronata, *Institutiones,* III, 549.

[99] *Cf.* Canon 1939, §§ 1 and 2. While the case under consideration does not constitute matter for a criminal process, yet Canon 1939 may rightfully be invoked to indicate the norm to be followed.—Noval, *De Processibus,* Pars. III, 582.

be taken immediately because of rumors or denunciations received from either priests or the laity; but rather the deans, priest-visitors, and prudent laymen should be consulted, as well as other means that might suggest themselves in particular instances, and all the testimonial evidence and proof should be reduced to writing in the event of recourse to the S. Congregation of the Council[100]

Once the proof of negligence is established, the ordinary must admonish the pastor, that is, he must call to his attention those obligations to teach Christian doctrine which are to be fulfilled. This admonition is strictly canonical, not in the sense of merely a penal remedy,[101] but rather of a coercive measure which contains a threat of punishment for a *delictum iam consummatum.* The execution of the threat by the infliction of a canonical punishment may follow immediately upon a new transgression without the intervention of additional or repeated admonitions. Mention must of course be made of the imminent punishments to which the negligent pastor will be liable, lest *he be led to believe that no more than a paternal correction was intended.* Such punishments, vindictive in nature,[103] will include not only those that may have been established by particular law, but also those which the ordinary may impose *per modum praecepti peculiaris*; [104] only in an extreme case, because of great scandal or because of the special seriousness of the transgression, could the ordinary impose any punishment without first admonishing the pastor.[105]

This admonition may be given by the ordinary personally or by

[100] Muniz, *Procedimientos,* I, 659; Suarez, *De Remotione Parochorum,* p. 183.

[101] Canon 2307.

[102] Noval, *De Processibus,* III, 582.

[103] Coronata, *Institutiones,* III, 549.

[104] Muniz, *op. cit.,* I, 661.

[105] Canon 2222, § 1.

It is disputed (*Cf.* Coronata, *op. cit.*, III, 549, in nota) whether the vicar general may give this admonition *sine mandato speciali.* Because this is strictly a coercive act ordained immediately for the infliction of a punishment, the negative opinion is preferred. (*Cf.* Canon 2220, § 2.)

his delegate, and either orally or by letter.[106] If it is given orally, that is, in the presence of the pastor, it should be reduced to writing, or it may also be read from a previously prepared document. It must be witnessed by the chancellor or some official of the diocesan curia, as a qualified witness, or two witnesses that are acceptable in law.[107] If it is given by letter, a receipt of its delivery must be obtained as defined by canon 1719. Finally, it is required that evidence of this procedure be reduced to writing by the notary and the acts thus written be preserved in the diocesan archives.[108] These acts will include a signed statement by the ordinary that he made the admonition together with the manner, names of witnesses, and the effect produced; and the admonition itself as reduced to writing and signed by the ordinary, the pastor, and the witnesses, or an exemplar copy of the letter (in case this method was used) together with a receipt of its delivery.[109]

If the pastor corrects the abuses which have caused him to neglect the teaching of Christian doctrine, the process is ended; if not, then it must be continued according to canon 2183:

> Si parochus sese non emendaverit, Episcopus eum corripiat et aliqua congrua poena pro gravitate culpae puniat, postquam auditis duobus examinatoribus et facta parocho sese defendendi facultate, probatum iudicaverit praedicta paroecialia officia etiam atque etiam per notabile tempus in re gravis momenti praetermissa aut violata fuisse et eorundem omissiones aut violationes nulla justa causa excusari.

To proceed according to this canon, the ordinary once again must be morally certain that the pastor has failed to show any signs of

106 Canon 2143, § 1. These two methods exclude any other, for example, *per edictum* (publication in a newspaper or affixing it to the door of the church). This is evident from the canon itself, neither may any argument be deduced from Canon 20, because there is no similarity between this process and a judicial one where such a method is permitted (Canon 1720) in order to show publicly that contumacy exists. Moreover, the culpability of the negligence is of itself secret, and to publish it would both defame the pastor and scandalize the people without any necessity. Noval, *op. cit.*, III, 434, 435.

107 Canons 2143, § 1, and 1756-1758.

108 Canon 2142.

109 Canon 2143, § 2.

emendation in fulfilling those obligations concerning which he has been expressly warned. It is not necessary, however, that negligence extend over any notable period of time, but rather that there has been complete failure in giving the required religious instruction which cannot be justified by any reasonable cause.[110] If proper amendment had been made, and only after a long period of time, negligence has once again become evident, then it would be necessary to revert to the beginning of the process as outlined above.[111] A further question presents itself which may be illustrated by the following case: Suppose a pastor had been warned of his negligence to instruct the children for their first Communion. He makes proper amendment, but in doing so, neglects to instruct the youth any further as required by canon 1331. Can the ordinary proceed to "correct and punish" according to canon 2183, or must he rather first admonish him according to canon 2182? Noval [112] holds that the ordinary may act according to canon 2183, and gives as his reason that it is the *mala voluntas* of the pastor which is the object of the punishment. The contrary opinion, which seems to offer as its reason the fact that the delicts are of a diverse species, maintains that the canonical admonition must be repeated.[113] The latter opinion is preferred because of the general rule: *in poenis benignior est interpretatio facienda.*[114]

Two things must now be done, namely the pastor must be corrected (*eum corripiat*) and a penalty imposed. This correction, which is a penal remedy,[115] is a solemn reprehension of the pastor because of his failure to comply with the regulations respecting catechetical instruction as it is his duty to do. This is to be done before witnesses,

[110] Coronata, *Institutiones,* III, 550, 551; Suarez, *De Remotione Parochorum,* p. 185.

[111] This is only a general rule. It is left ultimately to the judgment of the ordinary to decide as the merits of the case justify. Suarez, *op. cit.,* p. 186.

[112] *De Processibus,* III, 582.

[113] *Seems* is used advisedly here, because the distinction is made between failure to give instruction and failure to visit and care for those who are ill. (Suarez, *De Remotione Parochorum,* p. 185.) However, the obligations of catechetical instruction are to be taken separately, and therefore it appears logical to apply these distinctions to the present question.

[114] Canon 2219, § 1.

[115] Canon 2308.

and the documentary evidence of such is to be preserved with the acts of the process.[116] The nature of the punishment to be imposed is left to the discretion of the ordinary as the gravity of the negligence demands. He may select one fixed by particular law which could be in the nature of the recitation of certain prayers, a retreat, a performance of certain works of mercy; [117] or one of those included in canon 2298, as for instance the prohibition of exercising the offices of the priesthood except in a certain church, or a temporary suspension; or it may be one which the ordinary has determined *per modum praecepti particularis.*

This correction and punishment is conditioned on conclusive proof that the pastor has been culpable in his failure to fulfill the duties that are required. Therefore he is allowed every right to defend himself. This defense may be presented either orally or in writing, but in the former case it must be reduced to writing. In presenting his arguments, he is allowed the greatest freedom: he may directly attack the alleged reasons for his negligence to show that they are false; or show that the negligence is not to be regarded as being serious; or that it has not been present for any length of time; or that those who have accused him were prompted by unjust motives; or that there were just causes to excuse him. Only after the pastor has presented his case will the ordinary hear the examiners who have been appointed to investigate the allegations. This hearing is placed after the defense in order that the examiners may be able to estimate their evidence more accurately as well as rightly to advise the ordinary.[118] While their vote is merely consultative, nevertheless it is necessary for the validity of the process.[119]

If the pastor establishes his innocence, the case is ended. If the negligence is proven to be only slight, the ordinary should urge him to renew his efforts in giving proper instruction. In order to inflict both the penal remedy of correction and the punishment, three things must characterize the negligence, namely, the omission to teach Christian doctrine must have occurred frequently (*etiam atque*

[116] Canon 2309, §§ 3 and 5.

[117] Suarez, *op. cit.*, 188.

[118] Suarez, *op. cit.*, p. 186.

[119] Canon 105, 1°.

etiam); it must have continued over a sufficient length of time to indicate gross carelessness (*per notabile tempus*), and it must be concerned with a serious matter (*in re gravis momenti*), for instance, the failure to instruct children in preparation for their first Communion, or any other of the obligations associated with catechetical instruction since they are *officia gravissima.* However, it must be proved that these three essential requisites existed previous to the canonical admonition and that there has been no amendment after the admonition was given. Since, however, the pastor is afforded the opportunity of defending himself (which was denied him before the canonical admonition) and the case is argued in the presence of the examiners, these essential points, indicating negligence, must be thoroughly discussed and proved.[120]

If the pastor is repentant and promises to fulfill his duties, he is to be dispensed from the imposed penalties. If he is recalcitrant, then the case is continued according to canon 2184:

> Si et correptio et punitio in irritum cesserint, Ordinarius, probata, ad normam can. 2183, perseverante ac culpabili officiorum paroecialium omissione vel violatione in re gravi, parochum amovibilem sua paroecia statim privare potest; parochum vero inamovibilem beneficii fructibus, pauperibus ab Ordinario distribuendis, pro gravitate culpae in totum vel ex parte privet.

Once again it is absolutely necessary that culpable negligence has continued to exist in the failure to teach Christian doctrine. Therefore caution and prudence in judgment are required in examining the attendant circumstances, although it is not necessary that the violation of the catechetical precept has continued through a notable length of time. As defined in canon 2183, proof must be established in presence of the examiners with the right reserved to the pastor of defending himself.

After it is clearly proved that the pastor has persisted in his culpable failure to fulfill the duties incumbent upon him, the ordinary may remove a removable pastor from his parish immediately, notwithstanding the stability which the law has given him. From the word *potest* as used in the canon, it seems that the ordinary is not

[120] Suarez, *De Remotione Parochorum,* pp. 187, 188.

obligated to remove the pastor unless, other means being ineffective, it becomes imperative because of the good of the souls in the parish.[121] Because of the stability of the office of irremovable pastor,[122] the ordinary may not remove him immediately. He may, however, deprive him, in whole or in part, of the income from his benefice, which in turn is to be given to the poor. But if this proves ineffectual in removing contumacy, then the ordinary may remove such a pastor also from his office, according to canon 2185:

> Mala voluntate persistente ac probata, ut supra, Ordinarius etiam parochum inamovibilem e sua paroecia removeat.

In this instance also it must be conclusively demonstrated, according to the method already indicated, that the negligence has persisted. Proof being established, however, the pastor must be removed by the ordinary, who in this instance does not seem to be allowed any other method of procedure.

Removal, in both instances, is equivalent to the *punishment of deprivation,* since the process, which is a penal one, is complete in itself and independent of those processes[123] whose specific purpose is rather the *fact of removal* from office apart from any penal measure, and which thus constitute procedures which do not take into consideration the criminal causes, etc. Therefore, *per se,* the ordinary is not bound to provide for the pastor whom he has penally deprived of office in the same manner as he is urged to do for the one whom he has merely removed from office for reasons of ineffective parochial administration, as contemplated in canon 2154. However, if the pastor is not able to care for himself, both Christian charity and the honor of the sacerdotal office would demand that some kind of equitable provision be made for him.[124]

[121] Suarez, *De Remotione Parochorum,* p. 189. Noval, (*De Processibus,* III, 583) seems to indicate that the ordinary is allowed no alternative but that of immediate removal, but this appears to be too strict an interpretation of the word *potest.*

[122] Canon 454, § 2.

[123] Tit. XXVII: *De modo procedendi in remotione parochorum inamovibilium,* Canons 2147-2156; and Tit. XXVIII: *De modo procedendi in remotione parochorum amovibilium,* Canons 2157-2161.

[124] Muniz, *Procedimientos,* I, 659; Suarez, *op. cit.,* p. 190.

(b) Punishment of Priests and Other Clerics

The ordinary may also inflict punishment on those priests and other clerics who refuse, without a just cause, to assist their pastor in giving catechetical instructions.[125] It does not seem, however, that they could be punished for refusing to assist *any* pastor, unless it had been determined otherwise by particular law. Before inflicting punishment the ordinary must canonically warn the priest or cleric of his obligation and also of the punishment to be inflicted.[126] The nature of these punishments is left to the ordinary to determine. For priests, it will be either some penal remedy or vindictive punishment, while other clerics should not be promoted to higher orders.

(c) Punishment of Religious

The basis of the ordinary's powers to punish religious is canon 619, which states that "in all things in which religious are subject to the bishop they may also be punished by him with ecclesiastical penalties." By reason of canon 1336, all religious, even such as enjoy exemption,[127] must observe the diocesan regulations governing catechetical instruction. Therefore, whenever there is culpable negligence or carelessness in failure to observe these regulations, the ordinary of the diocese may proceed to inflict the proper punishment.[128] For example, in parishes conducted by religious, the pastors

[125] Canon 1333, § 2.

[126] *Cf. supra*, p. 68; Canon 2222, § 1.

[127] Schäfer, *De Religiosis*, p. 613.

[128] In applying Canon 619, the bishop *per se* is able to proceed both by way of vindictive penalties and censures, and this includes both non-exempt religious and exempt religious, Regulars not excepted. (Ballerini-Palmieri, *Opus Theologicum Morale*, VII, n. 77; Wernz-Vidal, *Jus Canonicum*, III, 436.) By virtue of a special privilege granted to Regulars, and those who participate in their privileges, the bishop *per accidens* is not able to apply censures except in such instances for which he is granted special authorization by way of exception to the privilege. Catechetical instruction seems to be one of these exceptions, from the following response of the S. Congregation of the Council: "An Episcopus possit cum censuris procedere contra Regulares exemptos, si inobedientes fuerint . . . in praedicatione verbi Dei, et hoc an vigore Concilii Tridentini, vel per quem Canonem?—*Respondit posse procedere,* non quidem in vim Concilii Tridentini, sed in vim Constitutionis Gregorii XV, quae incipit: Inscrutabili Dei providentia." (Piatus Montenses, *Praelectiones Juris Regularis,* II, q. 13.)

are directly subject to the diocesan regulations and may be punished by the ordinary for failure to fulfill them;[129] likewise in their primary and secondary schools and colleges, failure to use the prescribed texts and methods would justify punishment by the ordinary, since this phase of instruction is under his surveillance.[130] However, in those instances in which the ordinary, according to canon 1334, should request assistance from the religious superior, he is not able to enforce this assistance by means of canonical punishment, because he has no power to do so.[131]

(d) Punishment of Parents

The ordinary may also punish parents who fail in their obligations toward their children. For the sake of convenience, treatment of this is reserved to Chapter V.

Article 6. Pertinent Questions

It falls within the present discussion to consider some questions of practical moment relative to the instruction of non-Catholics. True, there is the obligation of preaching the Gospel to every creature, but the consideration here is rather linked with the possible canonical obligations arising from canon 1336. The basis of these would seem to be established by the word *populum,* which the canon uses without any modification. Since canon 1336 is mandatory, it would seem to follow logically that the ordinary is to lay down certain norms for the instruction of non-Catholics.

(a) Instruction of Non-Catholics for Marriage With Catholics

This question is considered first because such marriages afford immediate contact with non-Catholics. The point of view in this instance, however, is not to regard these instructions merely as a means of insuring the fulfillment of the ante-nuptial promises,[132] but in the exact sense of catechetics, namely to teach Christian doc-

[129] Canon 631, § 1, and Canon 471, § 4.
[130] S. C. C., decr., *Provido sane,* Jan. 12, 1935—*AAS,* XXVII (1935), 151.
[131] Coronata, *Institutiones,* II, 257.
[132] Canon 1061, § 1, 2°.

trine to those ignorant of the truths of Faith, with a view to their possible conversion. And thus the ordinary would determine both the number of instructions and the manner in which they are to be given. The fact that in many dioceses, in the United States especially, these instructions are given could be taken as an indication at least that ordinaries regard such regulations as mandatory.

However, such a course is not without difficulties, because often enough the non-Catholic party (as is understandable) cannot be made to appreciate or understand the real purpose of these instructions, and as a consequence, declines to take them. The question thus arises: "Can the ordinary prescribe these instructions as a condition for granting the dispensation?" In other words, can the ordinary refuse the dispensation if the non-Catholic party should refuse to take the prescribed instructions? And if he does grant the dispensation, there is the further question of having its validity depend upon the reception of these instructions. Possible arguments affirming might be adduced from two sources: First, because refusal to take these instructions would be sufficient proof to remove the required moral certitude that the ante-nuptial promises will be fulfilled; and second, because of canon 1039, which gives the ordinary power to prohibit a marriage temporarily for a just cause, which in this instance would be the refusal to take instructions. In response to the first argument, it may be said that while such a possibility must be admitted in extreme instances, *per se,* there is no repugnance between the sincerity to fulfill the promises and the refusal to take the required instructions. Likewise canon 1039 refers rather to intended marriages, which in their celebration or contraction raise no doubt or difficulty relative to validity, but which prompt a temporary delay for such just causes as the reasonable objection of parents, the fear of serious quarrels, and the like.[133] The impossibility of making such instructions a condition for granting a dispensation or having the validity of the dispensation depend on them, can be proved from the nature of the faculties by which the ordinary dispenses, for such faculties are delegated and in them there is no mention of any instructions to be given before the granting of a dispensation either

133 Vermeersch-Creusen, *Epitome,* II, 185.

from the impediment of mixed religion or that of disparity of cult.[134] Therefore, if such a condition were placed by the ordinary, it would be in excess of his delegated powers and of no effect.[135]

(b) *Instruction of Non-Catholics Apart From Marriage*

Two possibilities present themselves under this consideration. In the first place, there are those non-Catholics who of their own volition desire to take instructions. According to canon 752, they are not to be baptized until they have been thoroughly instructed. Therefore, it would seem that the ordinary is to prescribe the necessary conditions, not only by virtue of canon 1336, but also to establish uniformity throughout the diocese and to prevent carelessness and other abuses that might arise. Such regulations would include the minimum number of instructions required, the subject-matter to be learned, and such other things as, for instance, attendance at Sunday Mass, which the ordinary would judge as prudent. In the second place, there is the question of affording a general opportunity to all non-Catholics. In other words, must the ordinary provide, for example, that in each parish of the diocese publicly advertised classes in Christian doctrine be given at stated times during the year, in order both to stimulate a greater missionary activity in the various parishes as well as to afford non-Catholics an opportunity of studying the teachings of the Church? A peremptory answer can scarcely be deduced from the canonical precept, although the possibility of non-attendance would not seem to constitute a sufficient reason why such

[134] S. C. E. Off., 22 Nov., 1934: *Facultates Quinquenniales,* Formula IV, n. 2, 3.

[135] Canon 203. De facultatibus pro dispensationibus matrimonialibus ea lege a Vic. App. suis missionariis communicatis, ut debeant ipsi, sub poena nullitatis concessae dispensationis, schedulam tradere sponsis declarativam dispensationis elargitae, et dispensationem ipsam adnotare in regesto parochi, *observandum occurit quod notissimi juris est, non posse inferiorem coarctare absque venia superioris concessionem istius.* Igitur quas in foliis facultates habent Vicarii Ap. communicabiles suis missionariis vel in totum vel in partem possunt quidem eos communicare vel non communicare juxta datam sibi a Summo Pontifice auctoritatem, *sed minime possunt novas apponere conditiones et irritantes clausulas in iisdem communicandis,* quando ad sic agendum specialem non obtinuerint facultatem a S. Sede . . . S. C. P. F., litt. (Ad Vic. Ap. Tunk. Occid.), March 16, 1865. —Coll. S. C. P F, n. 1270.

prescriptions should not be made. In fact, such a provision has been incorporated in the synodal statutes of the archdiocese of San Francisco, which requires that instruction classes be held in each parish twice a week for converts.[136]

[136] No. 330: "Acatholicis quoque opportunitatem accipiendi de vera religione instructionem in unaquaque paroecia provideri oportet; ideo bis saltem in hebdomada habendi sunt pro convertendis scholae seu classes in aula paroeciali."—Statuta Archidioecesis Sancti Francisci (1936), pp. 81, 82.

CHAPTER IV

THE OBLIGATION OF PASTORS

Article 1. The Nature of the Obligation

Canon 1329: Proprium ac gravissimum officium, pastorum praesertim animarum, est catecheticam populi christiani institutionem curare.

Canon 467, § 1: Debet parochus . . . maximam curam adhibere in catholica puerorum institutione.

One of the most serious duties that is imposed on the pastor of a parish is to provide for the religious instruction of its members, especially the children. As with local ordinaries, so also with pastors does canon 1329 define this pastoral duty. There is this distinction, however, that the obligation of the ordinary arises by reason of a divinely instituted office, while that of the pastor has its basis in an office established by ecclesiastical law, that is, the pastor is obliged directly by ecclesiastical law, and indirectly by divine law in as much as he participates in the work of the episcopal office.[1] As pastor, he is also bound in justice to direct his efforts toward the accomplishment of this ministry.

The use of the words *gravissimum* and *maximam* in the above canons likewise indicates clearly that, of the pastoral duties, none is more important than that of catechetical instruction. While it can scarcely be stated that it should take precedence over the other obligations of the pastorate, at the same time it is certain that it is not to be neglected in any way because of these. The reasons for the gravity of this obligation are evident, to wit, men must be instructed in order that they realize fully the purpose of their existence: [2] "Ex eius observatione (*i. e.*, instruction) aut neglectu salus vel

[1] Benedict XIV, litt. encycl., *Etsi minime*, Feb. 7, 1742, N. 2—*Fontes*, n. 324.

ruina animarum magna ex parte pendet;" [3] moreover many of the evils that afflict Christian society can be traced to the lack of religious and moral education.[4] The seriousness therefore of the obligations, however much neglected, that are imposed upon the laity as a consequence of the Church's duty to teach cannot be minimized by those having the care of souls even though many, like some of our Lord's own disciples,[5] should through weakness or lack of faith fall away.[6]

Article 2. The Extension of the Term *Parochus*

As defined by the Code, the pastor is a priest or moral person to whom a parish has been conferred in title with the obligation of caring for the souls therein under the authority of the ordinary of the place.[7] The law also includes under this office quasi-pastors and parochial vicars enjoying full parochial powers.[8] The former are those priests who are assigned to parishes in apostolic vicariates and prefectures. The latter include the *vicarius curatus*, the *vicarius oeconomus*, the *vicarius substitutus*, the *vicarius adiutor*, and the *vicarius cooperator*.[9] In general they are those priests who, in the name and place of the pastor, perform the parochial duties in the care of souls and in celebrating the divine offices.[10] While pastors and quasi-pastors are responsible for the fulfillment of all the catechetical precepts, the obligation of parochial vicars will correspond to the nature of the particular vicariate which they exercise. Therefore, it is necessary to consider each one specifically:

[2] ". . . it pleased God, by the foolishness of preaching, to save them that believe."—1 Cor. i. 21. "Faith then cometh by hearing; and hearing by the word of God."—Rom. x. 17.

[3] S. C. de Sem. et Stud. Univ., litt., Sept. 8, 1926—*AAS*, XVIII (1926), 453.

[4] Coronata, *Institutiones*, II, 253.

[5] John vi. 61.

[6] Vermeersch-Creusen, *Epitome*, II, 409.

[7] Canon 451, § 1.

[8] Canon 451, § 2, 1° et 2°.

[9] In order that *adiutores* and *cooperatores* be classified as pastors in law (*qui parochorum nomine in iure censentur*—Canon 899, § 3), it is to be noted that full parochial powers must be given them.

[10] Wernz-Vidal, *Jus Canonicum*, II, 796; DeMeester, *Compendium*, II, 330.

(a) If a parish is united *pleno jure* to a religious house, to a cathedral or collegiate chapter, or any other moral person, a vicar *(vicarius curatus)* must be appointed for the actual care of souls. To him exclusively belongs the care of souls with all the rights and duties as defined both by the common law and by diocesan statutes or those established by custom.[11] Consequently he is charged with the responsibility of providing for religious instruction according to the norms of the diocese.

(b) Administrators of parishes (*vicarii oeconomi*) are those appointed during the vacancy of a parish to supply for the pastor until such a one is appointed. *Per se,* the administrator is obliged to the fulfillment of all parochial duties, but since it is merely temporary, he is not to do anything which might prejudice the rights or the obligations of the pastor. Therefore, he must observe the precepts which determine the imparting of religious instruction, but should not of his own initiative introduce a program which the pastor might not possibly approve.[12]

(c) Substitutes *(vicarius substitutus)* are those who have been legitimately constituted to perform the parochial duties, either because the pastor is to be absent for a period exceeding a week, or because he has been compelled to leave suddenly, or because, having been deprived of his parish, he is appealing his case to the Holy See.[13] The substitute lawfully holds the place of the pastor in all that pertains to the care of souls, unless the ordinary or the pastor will have made certain reservations. Therefore, relative to catechetics, it is possible that such restrictions may be imposed, which the substitute is then obliged to observe.

(d) Adjutants *(vicarius adiutor)* are those who have been deputed by the local ordinary to assume the duties of the pastor, who, on account of some permanent cause as, for example, old age, mental debility, blindness, is not able satisfactorily to conduct the parish with its corresponding obligations.[14] Since the law defines a twofold manner of appointment according to the condition of the pastor,

[11] Canon 471, §§ 1 and 4; Canon 1425.

[12] Canon 472, § 1, and Canon 473, § 1; DeMeester, *op. cit.*, II, 333.

[13] Canons 474, 465, §§ 4-6; 1923, § 2.

[14] Canon 475, §§ 1 and 2.

the adjutant's obligations relative to teaching Christian doctrine will follow the nature of the appointment. If the pastor is completely disabled, the appointee will have full parochial powers which are considered as ordinary.[15] If the pastor is only partially disabled, the rights and obligations of such an adjutant will be determined either by the letters of appointment, or by custom, or by the diocesan statutes. Especially from the letter of deputation will his obligations be determined, and therefore, that of catechizing.[16]

(e) Assistants *(vicarius cooperator)* are those who aid the pastor in the administration of the parochial duties. In so doing they are bound by the obligation of residence within the parish.[17] They enjoy only delegated powers which are determined in most instances by the pastor. Since they have received the *missio canonica* from the bishop to engage in the ministry of preaching, the pastor should not withhold his permission to exercise this, although strictly speaking, if the good of souls should demand it, he may do so. This permission, however, either express or tacit, must be obtained. The obligations of assistants include the pastoral care of the parishioners as often as it is reasonably requested either by the pastor or by the parishioners themselves. These obligations rest upon the basis of charity in favor of souls and of obedience due to superiors as well as of justice, which demands by way of implied contract, a bestowal of service in exchange for the emoluments received. While diocesan law may more accurately determine the duties of an assistant as they relate to catechetical instruction,[18] nevertheless certain rules are given as a guide by commentators: Some obligations are so proper to the pastor that he cannot delegate them to his assistants, unless he himself is legitimately impeded from fulfilling them personally; other duties do not bind so rigorously that he cannot delegate them. Of the former, the responsibility of directing and organizing parish classes in Christian doctrine is a part. Therefore, the assistants as

[15] Canon 873, § 1.

[16] Canon 475, § 3; DeMeester, *op. cit.*, II, 337; Wernz-Vidal, *op. cit.*, II, 802.

[17] Canon 471, 2°; Canon 476, §§ 5-7.

[18] For example, the assistant's obligation to give catechetical instruction is expressly defined by a statute of the Archdiocese of San Francisco: "Vicarius cooperator obligatione tenetur . . . pueros puellasque diligenter in catechesi instituere." No. 91, *Statuta Archidioecesis Sancti Francisci* (1936), p. 21.

indicated above, cannot assume this task without the permission of the pastor; and neither can the pastor delegate this office, unless he is legitimately impeded from fulfilling it. The reason for this is not so much to deny the assistant any rights, but rather to indicate that the pastor does not and can not fulfill his own proper obligations by simply delegating them to the assistants. A pastor's lawful absence from the parish, the extended size of the parish both in numbers and in territory, a personal state of sickness or a condition of ill health, and other similar causes would constitute legitimate impediments in view of which a pastor *could* rightfully call upon his assistants to render the aid necessary for the fulfillment of his obligations. It does not seem, however, that the weight of other parochial duties would be a legitimate impediment, since that of catechetics and its supervision is one of the most important pastoral duties. At all times the pastor is to see to it that the instructions are properly given, and to guard against abuses that might creep in.[19]

Included in this consideration also are rectors of churches *(rectores ecclesiae)* and chaplains. The former are those to whom has been entrusted the care of certain churches which are neither parochial, nor capitular, nor annexed to a religious community. Chaplains of women religious and of men religious of a lay institute, or a confraternity or pious association, as well as chaplains of prisons, hospitals, orphan asylums, and other pious houses bear a close relationship in law to the rectors of churches, especially as regards rights and duties.[20] Rectors of churches may be obligated by the ordinary, even under threat of punishment if necessary, to give catechetical instruction to those parishioners who live at too great a distance from the parochial church to be able conveniently to attend the parish classes.[21] Chaplains of religious houses are governed by special canons, which exclude them from any consideration here. All other chaplains, however, may be required by the ordinary to give instruction, as long as it would not interfere with their principal duties.

[19] DeMeester, *Compendium,* II, 340-346; Wernz-Vidal, *Jus Canonicum,* II, 803-805.

[20] Canon 479, §§ 1 and 2; Wernz-Vidal, *op. cit.,* II, 806, 807.

[21] Canon 483.

In conclusion, it remains to be pointed out that all priests are obligated in a certain manner by charity to give their efforts to religious instruction as far as circumstances will allow.[22] It is defined by law[23] that pastors are to seek their assistance, as well as that of other clerics, especially when they live in the parish; these in turn must respect this request and coöperate as far as is possible. Unjustified refusal to do so may be punished by the ordinary.

Article 3. Parochial Organization

Closely associated with diocesan organization of religious instruction is that of parochial organization. In order to facilitate the program for this instruction as outlined by the decree *Provido sane*, norms were also laid down which outline the framework for organization to be adopted in all parishes.[24] This is effected by coöperation between the pastor and the diocesan catechetical office; but even in those instances where the establishment of the latter has been justly impeded, parochial organization must be cared for.

The most important unit which is to be established in the parish is the Confraternity of Christian Doctrine, according to the prescription of canon 711, § 2. Its membership is to include all persons who are capable of teaching catechism and of assisting in the promotion of such instruction, especially school teachers who in virtue of their training are particularly qualified to engage in this work. To be erected as a confraternity, a formal decree of the ordinary

[22] Coronata, *Institutiones*, II, 253.

[23] Canon 1333, §§ 1 and 2. A further indication that seminary students should assist in catechetical work during their summer vacation is had in an instruction of the S. Congregation of the Sacraments (Dec. 27, 1930): "Ad Rmos locorum Ordinarios De Scrutinio Alumnorum peragendo antequam ad ordines promoveantur." In a questionnaire to be filled in by the pastor, it is asked whether the candidate for orders has applied himself to teaching Christian doctrine: "Num christianae doctrinae tradendae, quatenus huic extra Seminarium addictus fuerit, suam operam navet? (Priusquam vero candidatus ad ulteriores sacros Ordines promoveatur, si nondum praefato munere addictus fuerit, addici debet.)"—*AAS*, XXIII (1931), 122.

[24] "Quo vero eadem ipsa facilius in toto Orbe terrarum in effectum deducantur, haec Sacra Congregatio, probante SSmo. D. N. Pio PP. XI, in omnibus dioecesibus exsequenda mandat quae sequuntur."—*AAS*, XXVII (1935), 149.

must be issued to indicate this; [25] and once it is canonically erected, it is *ipso jure* aggregated to the Archconfraternity whose center is the Church of Santa Maria del Pianto in Rome.[26] As such, therefore, the Confraternity of Christian Doctrine may be defined as an organic [27] sodality, canonically erected, whose specific purpose is both to assist in teaching Christian doctrine and to aid in the promotion of the parochial catechetical program.[28]

The position of women as members of the Confraternity of Christian Doctrine causes no difficulty. That such a difficulty may arise, however, is due to the wording of the second paragraph of canon 709 in which it is stated that women may *only (tantum)* be enrolled in *a* confraternity in order to gain the indulgences and other special benefits that have been granted to the members *(confratibus)*. Because of this, Vromant [29] holds that *per se* women would thus be excluded from the meetings *(comitia)* and from the right of election.[30] This does not apply to the Confraternity of Christian Doctrine, however, for in the *Statuto della Venerabile Arciconfraternita della*

[25] Canon 708. For formularies of the Decree of Erection, *cf.* Prindiville, *The Confraternity of Christian Doctrine*, p. 80; Canon 686, §§ 1 and 2.

[26] Canon 711, § 2. By this aggregation all the indulgences, privileges, and other spiritual benefits which have been granted to the Archconfraternity by the Holy See are communicated to the Confraternity (Canon 722). A list of these will be found in Supplement I.

[27] By "organic" is meant that the Confraternity has its officers, rightly elected, whose duty it is to govern and provide that the by-laws regulating its internal discipline and activity are enforced.—Vromant, *De Fidelium Associationibus*, p. 12.

[28] Vromant, *op. cit.*, pp. 87 and 116.

[29] *De Fidelium Associationibus*, pp. 38, 88 and 94.

[30] Canon 715, § 1. By reason of Canon 709, § 2, women would seem to be excluded, however, from an active participation in the religious functions (709, §1) of the Confraternity of Christian Doctrine. This opinion, however, is uncertain; for the concept of a confraternity in the present practice of the Church, despite the apparent clarity of the law, seems to be given a rather wide interpretation (except in those countries where it still maintains a strict collegiate character, *viz.*, in Italy, Portugal, and certain parts of France) and in view of this women might possibly be permitted some form of participation in the religious functions, depending of course on what will be their exact nature—Beringer-Steinen, *Die Ablässe*, II, 11.

Dottrina Cristiana [31] issued in 1928, women are permitted an active membership, *i.e.*, with a right to participate in the meetings, to vote, to hold office, as well as engage in the work of the Confraternity: no distinction is made between men and women as to membership in the parochial unit; [32] moreover it is explicitly stated that the governing council is to be composed of the pastor as the director and others selected from clerics and persons of both sexes.[33] Finally a rescript of the S. Congregation of the Council, sent to the Bishop of Great Falls, Montana, expressly states that all (without distinction between men and women) may be members of the Confraternity of Christian Doctrine who are suitable for the work, and at the same time approves of the present organization in the United States in which women play an important part.[34]

[31] Facultate Nobis concessa a fel. rec. BENEDICTO Papa XV in audientia diei 18 decembris 1915, Constitutiones Archisodalitatis Doctrinae Christianae ad mentem ipsius Sanctitatis Suae, decreto diei 25 martii 1916 adprobavimus. Cum autem post promulgationem Codicis Iuris Canonici necessarium fuerit praescripta de facultate aggregandi Sodalitates alias Doctrinae Christianae immutare, Constitutiones sic reformatas et quadraginta tribus articulis distinctas adprobamus. Volumus autem ut singula in eis praescripta ab omnibus ad quos pertinuerit integre sancteque serventur ut salutare opus christianae institutionis Romanae plebis maiores in dies fructus proferat ad religionis et societatis bonum.

Datum Romae, ex Aedibus Vicariatus die 30 januarii, 1928.

Basilius Card. Vicarius.

F. Can. Pascucci, Secretarius.

[32] "A norma del Codice di Diritto Canonico in ogni parrocchia deve essere eretta la Congregazione della Dottrina Cristiana. Essa si compone di tutti coloro che con l'opera e con i mezzi coadiuvano il parroco per l'insegnamento della Dottrina cristiana . . ."—*Statuto,* Art. 35.

[33] "I membri del Consiglio potranno scegliersi tra gli ecclesiastici e fra le persone di *ambo i sessi,* che con lodevole premura si prestano nelle varie opere della parrocchia e specialmente tra coloro che, accostando per ufficio o per dovere di carita le famiglie, possono piu facilmente adoperarsi per il fine delle Congregazioni parrocchiali."—*Statuto,* Art. 37.

[34]

"Romae, die 10 julii 1936
"S. Congregatio Concilii
"Officium Catechisticum

"Exme ac Revme Domine,

"Quae ex relatis huic S. Congregationi Concilii postremis hisce temporibus ab Ordinariis Foederatorum Americae Septemptrionalis Statuum peracta fuisse con-

Religious also may be enrolled as members, provided that the laws of the Confraternity do not conflict with the observance of the religious constitutions and rules.[85] Since judgment concerning this conflict pertains to the religious superior, his permission is required in order to join.[86] Because this privilege is accorded to religious by the common law, such permission, *servatis servandis,* should not be denied.[87] Even in the instance where membership would conflict with the religious discipline, religious may participate in the spiritual benefits granted to the Archconfraternity provided that they teach

stat ad religiosam populi christiani institutionem magis magisque fovendam, haec libenter eadem S. Congregatio perspecta habuit et perpendit.

"Prae ceteris, utillimum ad optatum finem assequendum procul dubio visum est quod Episcoporum Coetus Confraternitatibus doctrinae christianae provehendis, provido quidem consilio, constituit et decrevit quod nempe in unaquaque paroecia, pro rerum locorumque adiunctis, ad normam canonis 711, § 2, Codicis J. C. et decreti huius S. Congregationis diei 12 januarii 1935 Confraternitas seu Sodalitas doctrinae christianae institueretur.

"Quae Confraternitates, uti ex actis huic S. Congregationi transmissis cognoscere fas est, in hoc praecipuum munus intendunt *ut omnes simul complectantur quotquot in singulis paroeciis catechismo docendo et fovendo sunt idonei,* quique sollicita cura et statuta methodo pueros adolescentesque omnes catechisticam institutionem edoceant.

. . .

"Haec autem cum in Audientia diei 7 julii curr. Pio PP XI retulissem, idem SS.mus D.nus et de iis quae hactenus acta sunt et de agendis isti Episcoporum Coetui vehementer gratulari dignatus est, atque vota depromere ut tam feliciter incepta prospere cedant. Hunc in finem, et in signum Suae benevolentiae memoratis Episcopis necnon omnibus qui doctrinae christianae impensius curandae et provehendae operam navant, Apostolicam Benedictionem impertiri quoque dignatus est.

"Hanc nactus occasionem, quo par est obsequio me profiteor.

"Exmo ac Revno Domino
"Dno EDVINO O'HARA
"Episcopo GREAT-ORMENSI
"Praesidi Coetus Episcoporum
"Confraternitatibus doctrinae
"christianae provehendis."

"Excellentiae Tuae Rev.mae
"uti fratrem
"J. card. Serafini
"praefectum

For the approved constitution of parish units of the Confraternity of Christian Doctrine, *cf.* Supplement III.

85 Canon 693, § 4.

86 Schäfer, *De Religiosis,* p. 812.

87 Vromant, *op. cit.,* p. 38.

Christian doctrine in the parish, or in their schools and colleges.[38]

A threefold function is defined by the Statutes of the Confraternity: [39] Its members are to encourage parents and those who occupy the place of parents to send their children to the parish classes; in the conduct of the latter, the members are to supervise them in order to maintain order and discipline; and finally they are to provide those means that are necessary for the development of the course in religious instruction. In addition, the statutes regulating the activity of the Confraternity in a particular parish are to be adapted to existing conditions. For example, its activities will vary depending on whether the parish has a complete school unit or not; similarly, if the parish has only a grade school but no high school. Another factor will be whether all children of the parish attend the parochial schools, or whether some are impeded from doing so for a just cause, as for instance, because they live at too great a distance from the school, because they must work at home, and the like. These illustrate how the objectives of the Confraternity in a particular parish will be determined by local circumstances, but it must be noted that its constitution should have the approval of the local ordinary.[40] Finally, it is to be observed that while the statutes define a threefold function for the Confraternity, they do not restrict the members from teaching Christian doctrine.[41] Especially are they to do so when the pastor, because of some legitimate impediment, is unable to fulfill this task personally or only with great difficulty. This is determined by canon 1333, which states:

[38] "I religiosi e le religiose che impartono l'insegnamento catechistico in parrocchia o nei loro Istituti e Collegi, sono considerati come cooperatori nel territorio parrocchiale dell' opera catechistica, e possono, senza alcun detrimento delle loro costituzioni, lucrare le sante indulgenze, qualora il loro Istituto o Casa religiosa ne abbia ottenuta la partecipazione dall' Arciconfraternita della Dottrina Cristiana."—*Statuto,* Art. 34.

[39] Tit. V, Art. 38—*Statuto,* p. 14.

[40] Vromant, *op. cit.,* p. 116.

[41] Father Prindiville has described the work of the Confraternity of Christian Doctrine as it is carried on in certain dioceses in the United States, including Pittsburgh, Brooklyn, Los Angeles, San Diego, Santa Fe, Monterey-Fresno, Great Falls, and Helena.—Prindiville, *The Confraternity of Christian Doctrine,* pp. 35-51.

> **Parochus in religiosa puerorum institutione . . . debet operam adhibere . . . si necesse sit, piorum laicorum, potissimum illorum qui in pium sodalitium *doctrinae christianae* aliudve simile in paroecia erectum adscripti sint.**

When members of the laity are engaged to teach, however, they must be qualified to do so. In the first place, they should have the necessary intellectual ability, that is, sufficient knowledge both of Christian doctrine and of the prescribed methods. Since their selection belongs to the pastor, it is his duty to see that they have these qualifications, and if necessary, to instruct them further in the subject-matter which they are to teach. Moreover, the diocesan catechetical office, as noted above,[42] is to issue each year a special set of lectures on some particular topic for teachers.[43] Secondly, catechists should reflect the moral virtues in their lives so that by example they may inspire those intrusted to their care. Especially should they be motivated by a deep love of God, from which flows not only zeal, patience, and prudence—virtues so essential for a successful catechist—but also tact in the use of proper textbooks and methods of teaching.[44]

By using the word *laicorum,* the canon does not refer to men alone, but also to women. In part this gives support to the position of women in the Confraternity of Christian Doctrine as being able to teach. This was specifically declared in pre-Code law, and this interpretation of the word *laicorum* remains.[45] This is confirmed by the decree *Provido sane* and is taught by modern authors.[46]

[42] P. 54.

[43] In order to develop capable lay-teachers, Pope Pius XI has strongly urged that in all the principal educational centers conducted by religious, there should be established, under the leadership and direction of the bishops, special classes for a chosen group of young people of both sexes who shall be trained by a suitable course of studies to qualify for teaching Christian doctrine and sacred and ecclesiastical history: ". . . quod profecto fiet, si in scholis et collegiis catholicis, inter res pueris adolescentibusque addiscendas, principem locum habet, ut ratio ipsa suadet et postulat, institutio religiosa, quae et sacerdotibus docendo peritis, et apta instituendi ratione tradatur." S. C. C., decr., *Provido sane,* Jan. 12, 1935—*AAS,* XXVII (1935), 152.

[44] "Qualities of a Successful Catechist," *IER,* V (Series 1—1869), 472-479.

[45] Benedict XIV, litt. encycl., *Etsi minime,* Feb. 7, 1742, N. 7—*Fontes,* n. 324; Wernz, *Jus Decretalium,* III, 39.

[46] Vermeersch-Creusen, *Epitome,* II, 410; Blat, *Commentarium,* III, 257; Augustine, *Commentary,* VI, 346.

The Catholic Instruction League [47] has been established in many parishes also, especially in the United States. In the decree of erection it is classified as a Pious Union with the dignity of Primaria and the consequent perpetual right of aggregating other Unions of the same title and institute, which are canonically erected anywhere in the world, and to communicate to these all the indulgences which have been granted to this Instruction League, or which may hereafter be granted to it. The question of importance that arises is whether this Pious Union may be substituted for the Confraternity of Christian Doctrine, especially since the promulgation of the *Provido sane.* Previous to this decree, it was generally conceded that this substitution could be made even though canon 711, § 2, stipulates that the Confraternity is to be established in every parish. The reason given for this affirmative answer to the proposed question was that the League had received its approbation *after* the promulgation of the Code from the highest authority in the Church. The approbation thus given warranted the substitution of the Catholic Instruction League.[48] Since the more recent decree (*Provido sane*) on the establishment of the Confraternity of Christian Doctrine simply confirms canon 711, § 2, the above mentioned reason for the admissibility of the League provides for the present, also the basis of an affirmative answer relative to the permissibility of the latter's continued existence.

To complete the parish organization, classes in catechism are to be provided in which, under the guidance of the pastor and according to the prescribed method, children, young people, and adults are to be taught the rudiments of Christian doctrine. These classes are to be arranged according to the plan drawn up by the diocesan

[47] The Catholic Instruction League was established at Loyola University in Chicago, Ill., by John Lyons, S.J., in 1912, for the purpose of giving religious instruction to Catholic boys and girls who attend public schools. In addition, its aim is to instruct Negroes, Chinese, and others whose religious education has often been neglected, especially in the United States. Finally, it strives to be a timely and useful means for both Catholics and non-Catholics of good will who desire to become thoroughly instructed in the dogmas and moral principles of Catholicism.—Pius XI, brief, Aug. 5, 1925—Bouscaren, *The Canon Law Digest (Cumulative Supplement, 1935-1396),* pp. 67-69.

[48] "The Catholic Instruction League," *AER,* XCI (1934), 73-75.

office. They are to be conducted in a serious, orderly, and regular manner because of the importance of religious instruction and because of the children's tendency to evaluate the importance of anything from the manner in which it is treated. In other words, if the classes are conducted in a careless manner, if the subject-matter is presented in an obscure way, the children will be left with the impression that such instruction is unimportant and it will thus prove of little avail for future use and application. Moreover, pastors and those assisting them are to strive diligently to draw the children to the classes in religion by whatever means are most effective, for example, by having the students participate in solemnities on feast-days, by having contests, by offering prizes, and by allowing modest and reasonable recreation.

Article 4. Instruction of Children

The parochial unit affords, generally speaking, one of three possibilities: the parish church together with a primary (grade) school and secondary school (high school), the parish church with only a primary school, or the parish church with no school facilities whatsoever. Canons 1330 and 1331, which define the pastor's obligation as it pertains to religious instruction of children, are concerned only with the last two possibilities mentioned.[49] As is clear, this does not imply that in parishes where a complete school system is established the pastor is exempt from the supervision and teaching of catechism.[50] Even in these cases, the obligation remains as the most important of his parochial duties (canon 1329). But, since under such circumstances the law deals primarily with the subject of parochial schools, the exact nature and extent of the obligation here under discussion is not of direct concern, except to point out that it

[49] Coronata, *Institutiones*, II, 255. *Per accidens*, however, the first possibility is also included in the event that the school facilities will not accommodate all the children of the parish.

[50] "Praeceptores sacerdotali charactere non insigniti, sive religiosi sive laici, magno equidem sunt adjumento in juvenum institutione, at munus verbi Dei docendi sibi proprium non habent. 'Labia enim sacerdotis custodient scientiam, et legem requirent ex ore ejus.' "—*Acta et Decreta Concilii Plenarii Baltimorensis Tertii*, n. 217.

exists for the pastor as long as the ordinary of the place has not appointed other priests, according to canon 1373, § 2, fulfill this duty in the school system of a parish.

Previous to the Code the law [51] required that pastors of parishes were to instruct the children on *all* Sundays and holydays of obligation. As was indicated above,[52] this prescription of the pre-Code law no longer binds, although its directive force should not be completely discarded. Despite this fact, however, it must be kept in mind that it is precisely because of canon 6, n. 6 [53] that this opinion is sustained, and not because of the prescriptions of canons 1330 and 1331 which deal rather with specific circumstances, as will be seen. On the contrary, these laws presuppose that the youth of the parish have been taught in a general way the principal elements of Christian doctrine. It is on the occasion of the reception of the sacraments there indicated that a more thorough instruction, restricted to an explanation of these sacraments is required.[54] Thus it would seem that the Code is leaving it to the discretion of the ordinary rather to define on what days during the week the parish classes are to be held, than to indicate that continuous weekly classes are to be omitted entirely. Therefore the pastor will follow the diocesan regulations and formulate no contrary argument from the fact of the possible non-existence of such regulations because the law contemplates no such situation.

In the United States an important consideration is whether the decree of the Second Council of Baltimore, which requires classes to be held on Sundays and holydays of obligation still retains its binding force:

> Iidem (episcopi) etiam saltem dominicis et aliis festivis diebus pueros in singulis parochiis fidei rudimenta et obedientiam erga Deum et parentes diligenter ab iis (pastoribus,

[51] Conc. Trid., sess. XIV, *de ref.*, cap. 4; Pius X, litt. encycl., *Acerbo nimis*, April 15, 1905, N. 1—*Fontes*, n. 666.

[52] P. 51.

[53] "Si qua ex ceteris disciplinaribus legibus, quae usque adhuc viguerunt, nec explicite nec implicite in Codice contineatur, ea vim omnem amisisse dicenda est, nisi in probatis liturgicis libris reperiatur, aut lex sit iuris divini sive positivi sive naturalis."

[54] Noval, *De Processibus*, III, 578.

tum saecularibus tum religiosis), ad quos spectabit, doceri curabunt.[55]

If this is regarded simply as a particular law, it certainly remains in force [56] in as much as it is outside (*praeter*) any of the provisions of the common law. Consequently a just cause would be required for the ordinary to dispense from its obligation.[57] Such a position can scarcely be maintained, however; for this law is merely a restatement of the Tridentine provision [58] and since this has been abolished by the Code, the regulation of the Council of Baltimore suffers a like fate. There is an added argument to sustain this viewpoint from the fact that custom may have abolished this law in many dioceses of this country. It can be safely stated therefore that the local ordinary is free to determine specifically the days on which the children are to be instructed.

Canon 1330: Debet parochus:

1°. Statis temporibus, continenti per plures dies institutione, pueros ad sacramenta poenitentiae et confirmationis rite suscipienda singulis annis praeparare.

2°. Peculiari omnino studio, praesertim, si nihil obsit, Quadragesimae tempore, pueros sic instituere ut sancte Sancta primum de altari libent.

The first specified duty of the pastor is to prepare the youth of his parish in a *particular* manner for the reception of the sacraments of Penance, Holy Eucharist and Confirmation. This implies that these instructions are to be given in addition to the regular parish classes and that their immediate purpose is of a practical nature, namely, that the youth will thus receive these sacraments with a knowledge of their nature and importance. While the canon distinguishes instruction for each sacrament, it does not necessarily indicate that a period of time is to intervene in the reception of each. Penance and Holy Communion need not be separated. The age

55 *Concilii Plenarii Baltimorensis,* II, Acta et Decreta, n. 128.

56 Canon 6, § 1.

57 Canon 291, § 2.

58 Conc. Trid., sess. XXIV, *de ref.*, cap. 4.

for the reception of Confirmation under ordinary circumstances, as defined by the Code[59] and explained more fully by recent declarations of the Pontifical Commission for the interpretation of the Code[60] and the S. Congregation of the Sacraments[61] is around seven years, unless the custom of administering it before the age of reason obtains. Moreover, the S. Congregation of the Sacraments counsels that this sacrament, because it complements Baptism and bestows the fullness of the Holy Spirit, should be received before the children make their first Communion if at all possible, although the Congregation does not intend to bar the reception of first Holy Communion when a child has reached the age of discretion simply because Confirmation has not been previously received.

For this preparation the pastor is to instruct the children at fixed periods continuing through several days. The intention of the law here is twofold: namely, that for a certain number of days, joined at least by moral continuity, these preparatory instructions be given; and that not only once, but several times during the year opportunity be given for all to be instructed.[62] The designation of these periods belongs to the ordinary of the place and it is incumbent upon the pastor to conform to the arrangement made.[63] This annual preparation is to be provided in parishes for all the sacraments which are to be received in the course of the year. In parishes where Confirmation is not administered each year, the obligation of instructions on this sacrament is not imposed as an annual duty. This is the evident import of the canon. Finally, in the matter in which the children are to be instructed, the pastor will likewise follow the diocesan regulations relative to the manner and subject-matter of the instructions corresponding to the age and condition of the students.

It is evident from the wording of the law that the pastor is obliged to intensify the tenor and elaborate the content of his instruction when preparing the children of the parish for first Communion. In designating Lent as the period for this instruction the

[59] Canon 788.

[60] Cod. Com., June 16, 1931—*AAS*, XXIII (1931), 353.

[61] S. C. de Sacr., June 30, 1932—*AAS*, XXIV (1932), 271.

[62] Noval, *De Processibus*, III, 578.

[63] Vermeersch-Creusen, *Epitome*, II, 409.

Code insinuates that this is the time preferred to prepare children for their first Communion, because it better corresponds to the tradition of the Church.[64] However, it affords the opportunity of selecting a more suitable time, in case there should be reason to do so. From the words *si nihil obsit,* it would seem that some reasonable or equitable cause is required for deviating from the recommended time. Among such causes could be enumerated the incapacity on the part of the pastor through sickness, or his legitimate absence from the parish; reasonable grounds, such as inclement weather, heavy roadways and arduous walking, which may be urged in excuse for non-attendance; opportunity to provide more suitable instruction at other times of the year; moral impossibility occasioned by the added work at mission-churches attached to the parish. The authors do not offer any special comment on this phrase. In view of this one may reasonably conclude that any equitable purpose will suffice for the selection of a different season of the year for this special course of instruction.

However, the prescriptions of the Third Council of Baltimore *per se* appear to retain their binding force relative to the preparations required for first Communion:

> Jubemus ergo ut parvulorum curam assiduam habeant animarum rectores, praesertim quo tempore parantur ad sacram synaxim prima vice recipiendam, et quidem ut ipsimet rectores vel eorum vicarii praedictos parvulos saltem per sex hebdomadas et ter in unaquaque hebdomada (saltem in loco ubi resident vel ad quem facilius accedere possunt) catechismum doceant.[65]

From this it is evident that not only at the parish churches where they reside, but also—if it is reasonably possible—at the subsidiary and filial churches within the parish limits, pastors shall prepare the children for their first Communion with instructions to be given three times a week for a period of six weeks, falling within the season of Lent in accordance with the preference expressed by the Code. Whenever no obstacle militates against it, the preference of Lent as indicated in the Code must be regarded as mandatory.

[64] Vermeersch-Creusen, *Epitome,* II, 409; Blat, *Commentarium,* III, 257.

[65] *Acta et Decreta Concilii Plen. Balt.*, n. 218.

In preparing the children for their first Communion, the pastor has the right and duty, as defined by the above canon, to instruct them personally, if this is possible. Here may be noted an apparent conflict that seems to exist between the position of the pastor and that of the parents as defined by canon 854, § 3, which designates the latter (together with the confessor) as the ones who are to determine whether or not their children have the necessary dispositions to receive their first Communion. A possible explanation of this, however, may be deduced from the fact that the first Communion of children (as prescribed by the decree *Quam singulari* [66]) was regarded as a purely private and individual matter and, as a result, the required preparation devolved quite naturally on the parents. In practice group instruction gradually became the accepted method, which is now entrusted by law (canon 1330, 2°) to the pastor, without prejudice, however, to the rights of the parents. In those instances, however, where parents instruct their children, the pastor has the duty of certifying, even by a previous examination if necessary, that the children have attained the use of reason, accompanied with a sufficient knowledge and the requisite dispositions and to be vigilant in guarding against the admission to first Holy Communion of children who lack these needed requisites.[67]

In the preparation of candidates for the Sacrament of Confirmation, the Third Council of Baltimore (n. 218) prescribed:

> Nemo ad confirmationis susceptionem admittatur, quin diligenter instruatur de iis, quae ad naturam effectumque hujus sacramenti spectant. Episcopum itaque, confirmationem adolescentibus collaturum hortamur ut confirmandos sive per se sive presbyterum in doctrina Christiana examinet.

Since this is in harmony with the Code it still continues in force.[68]

Canon 1331: Praeter puerorum institutionem de qua in Can. 1330, parochus non omittat pueros, qui primam communionem recenter receperint, uberius ac perfectius catechismo excolere.

[66] S. C. de Sacr., Aug. 8, 1910—*Fontes*, n. 2103.

[67] Canon 854, §§ 4 and 5.

[68] Barrett, *A Comparative Study of the Councils of Baltimore and the Code of Canon Law* (Washington, 1932), p. 165.

The first point of emphasis in regard to this canon is that it dispels and corrects the error which has existed in the minds of many Catholics that catechetical instruction ends with the making of one's first Communion. The law commands that children are to be instructed further after having received the necessary instructions for the reception of the sacraments prescribed by canon 1330. To what age these instructions are to be continued is to be determined by particular law. According to the custom which prevailed until recently in the United States, Confirmation was usually the last of the sacraments mentioned to be received. While the age varied somewhat, it may be stated with a fair amount of certainty that the average was from ten to twelve years and that instruction was continued up to this age. From the tenor of recent declarations of the Holy See, formal instruction is to be given until the student has completed his secondary (high school) education, and, even further, if he attends college.

The subject-matter is to be adapted to the literary and scientific culture which the students have by this time acquired. They should be taught how to defend the truths of Faith against objections, as well as how to explain them to others in a persuasive manner.[69] This determination of the subject-matter is left to particular law.

As a norm of interpretation of this canon, for the United States at least, the enactments of the fourth Provincial Council of Portland, Oregon, held in 1932, are important. For this reason, they are quoted here in their entirety:

> Curent Ordinarii locorum ut foveatur plenior religionis doctrina per associationes quae "Study Clubs" vocantur, praesertim pro iis qui, absoluto curriculo elementario vel medio, altiora studia non prosequuntur.[70]

For the students attending the public schools:

> Hujusmodi instructiones [more complete religious instructions] fiant bis, vel saltem semel, in hebdomada, durante toto anno scholastico, etiam pro iis iuvenibus qui

[69] Coronata, *op. cit.*, II, 255.

[70] Decr. 34—*Acta et Decreta Concilii Provincialis Portlandensis in Oregon Quarti*, p. 43.

> scholas superiores (high schools) publicas frequentant. In istis instructionibus sacerdotes ne omittant, ad normas ab Ordinario praescriptas, pueros puellasque monere contra pericula fidei et moribus adversantia. Pariterque sub moderamine Ordinarii loci eosdem bene praeparent ad refutandos errores falsae philosophiae moralis, pseudo-historiae, pseudo-scientiae, aliosve a quibusdam directe vel indirecte propositos in moderna acatholica iuventutis institutione.
>
> Invigilent Ordinarii adimplendis hisce praescriptis ne adolescentes erroribus supradictis seducti paulatim a Fide deficiant. Valde optamus ut in unaquaque dioecesi eligantur sacerdotes in scientia apologetica praestantes qui schemata instructionum proponant ad refellendos errores in falsa iuventutis institutione grassantes.[71]

For Catholic students in non-Catholic colleges and universities:

> Instituantur "Newman Clubs" in quibus iuvenes doctrina christiana eo solidius informentur, quo gravius incurrant periculum fidei amittendae.
>
> Removeatur quoque consortium discipulorum ex quo fides aut mores in discrimen adduci solent. (Epis. S. C. de Prop. Fide ad Archiep. Westmonasterien., 17 Apr. 1895).
>
> Sacerdotes destinentur idonei ad opus de quo supra promovendum, qui ne omittant omnibus quibus possint modis adolescentes et adolescentulas in Fide confirmare et sustinere.[72]

These decrees uphold the opinion that instruction is to be continued through the high school age of the students, and to be protracted for those attending colleges.

In summing up the obligation of pastors to instruct the youth of their parish, the decree of the Sacred Congregation of the Council admonishes thus:

> Let pastors and others having the care of souls always keep in mind that catechetical instruction is the foundation of the whole Christian life, and that all their prudence, study, and labor must be brought to bear in duly teaching it. Let them, therefore, correctly observe and perform those things which are prescribed by canons 1330 and 1331, and

[71] Decr. 33—*ibid.*, p. 42.

[72] Decr. 36—*ibid.*, p. 43. *Cf.* also the statutes (326-329) of the Archdiocese of San Francisco, pp. 80, 81.

1332 and, especially, let all things be carried out so that they may win all men for Christ, and be able to prove themselves faithful ministers and dispensers of the mysteries of God, thoughtfully considering for whom milk, for whom more solid food is necessary; and to each, let them serve the food of doctrine, which nourishes the spirit so that the Christian man, not only will not be ignorant of those things which pertain to religion, neither will he hold them as if transmitted by heredity, but also will have a well-grounded and thorough knowledge of them which will bear fruit for himself and others.[73]

Article 5. Instruction of Adults

Canon 1332: Diebus dominicis aliisque festis de praecepto, ea hora quae suo iudicio magis apta sit ad populi frequentiam, debet insuper parochus catechismum fidelibus adultis, sermone ad eorum captum accommodato, explicare.

This canon obligates pastors to instruct the adult members of their parishes in Christian doctrine. It thus emphasizes the distinction to be made between a sermon (*concio*) and instruction, and by this, indicates that the fulfillment of the former does not suffice for the fulfillment of the latter.

As has already been discussed this obligation does not bind strictly for every individual Sunday and holyday of obligation, but admits of occasional omission for reasonable causes. The number of days that instruction may thus be omitted is to be determined by particular law according to conditions as they exist in the various dioceses.

In this instruction of adults, a distinction must be made between those who lack all knowledge of Christian doctrine and those who have been instructed during youth according to the spirit of the above-mentioned laws. For the former group, it seems essential that they be instructed in separate classes after the manner of parish classes for children. For the latter, it seems that there can be no question of insistence on compulsory attendance at such study groups that

[73] S. C. C., decr., *Provido sane*, Jan. 12, 1935—*AAS*, XXVII (1935), 148.

may have been organized within the parish, although it is highly desirable that as many as possible attend wherever such an opportunity is offered. The greatest difficulty that arises in their regard is from the phrase *ea hora quae suo iudicio magis apta sit ad populi frequentiam* as used in the canon, and the question is whether this indicates that instruction is to be given at a time distinct from the Sacrifice of the Mass, for instance, either immediately before or after, or in the afternoon or evening. If by this explanation of the catechism the law (as judged from its context) intends a certain methodical treatment of the subject-matter wherein the people would take an active part (*i. e.*, by questions, discussions, etc.), then it would seem that instruction is to be given outside of the time for Mass. However, in using the word *explicare,* the canon seems rather to insinuate that only a more advanced instruction be given to the people who are already sufficiently grounded in the fundamentals of Christian doctrine, and therefore no active participation is necessary. This could be done during Mass. Because, moreover, it is left to the pastor's judgment to fix the time (and in the canon the hour of Mass is not explicitly excluded), the determining factor will be the actual ability of the parishioners to attend the instruction.[74] Therefore, it may be safely stated that instruction may be given during Mass, especially if the condition of the parishioners would prevent this from being done efficiently at any other time. Any conflict that would arise in this instance with the obligation of the sermon [75] may be avoided by omitting the sermon with the permission of the ordinary,[76] or even by

[74] Noval, *op. cit.,* III, 580; "Si instructio catechetica pro adultis, de qua in canone 1332, commode post meridiem fieri non potest, danda est intra Missam." *Synodus Roffiensis* (1934), n. 70.

[75] Canon 1344, § 1.

[76] Canon 1344, § 3. An indication at least of this possibility is had in a response of the S. Congregation of the Council, March 14, 1767, given to the vicar general of Cologne: a decree of the ordinary had allowed catechetical instruction for youth and adults to be substituted for sermons on the Wednesdays and Fridays of Lent. Because of this, the question was submitted: "An sustineatur ordinatio catechesis faciendae a parocho vel sacellanis pro erudiendis pueris ad Sacramenta paschalia, loco concionis quadragesimalis, feriis quarta et sexta in casu?" The Congregation approved because "conciones minorem utilitatem spiritualem conferunt, quam catechesis, qua et juventus et adulti ad digne suscipiendum SS. Sacramenta praeparantur. . . ."—*Fontes,* n. 3756.

having both a short well-prepared instruction and a sermon. Commentators are silent on this question.

In these instructions for adults, the pastor is to explain the subject-matter as it is given in the Catechism of the Council of Trent "in such a way as to cover in four or five years all the matter relating to the Creed, the Sacraments, the Ten Commandments, prayer, and the commandments of the Church," as well as the evangelical counsels, grace, the virtues, sin and the four last things.[77] It is evident from the very nature of things that these instructions are to be accommodated to the mental ability of the people.

Article 6. Specific Obligations

In addition to the laws regulating the instruction of children and adults, the Code has likewise specified certain instances in which instruction is to be given. Because of this, an explanation of these canons finds its proper place here. These obligations rest on the pastor, and only once is the ordinary of the place included, namely:

> **Canon 1405, § 2: Ordinarii locorum aliique curam animarum habentes opportune moneant fideles de periculo et damno lectionis librorum pravorum, praesertim prohibitorum.**

Ordinaries, pastors and assistants, and others charged with the care of souls, have the duty of warning the faithful against the dangers of reading perverse literature, especially prohibited books. The purpose of this law is to protect the faith and morals of the people so that the fruits of catechetical instruction will not suffer detriment from such a perfidious blight and that a vigorous Christian life will be constantly maintained. In order that the faithful may be directed correctly (*opportune*) in this matter, the laws of the Church should be explained, especially canon 1399, which enumerates the list of those publications that are condemned *ipso jure*. In this way, the faithful are able to judge for themselves the morality of various types

[77] S. C. C. decr., *Provido sane,* Jan. 12, 1935—*AAS,* XXVII (1935), 150. In requesting the use of the Tridentine Catechism, the meaning seems rather to indicate the use of those approved texts which are based on this Catechism.

of literature, and no temptation is afforded by expressly mentioning any book or publication. If, however, necessity should demand it, the ordinary may publicly prohibit a certain book, or announce that it has been prohibited by the Holy See.[78] Pastors and other priests should be vigilant in their care that books against faith or morals are kept out of the schools under their jurisdiction and endeavor also to keep such books out of public libraries.[79] In view of the baneful conditions existing today relative to publications, the weighty obligations of this canon may not be minimized or regarded lightly.

Canon 743: Curet parochus ut fideles, praesertim obstetrices, medici, et chirurgi, rectum baptizandi modum pro casu necessitatis probe ediscant.

Because Baptism is necessary *necessitate medii* for the salvation of all men,[80] pastors are obligated by this law of the Code to instruct the faithful, especially nurses and doctors, in the manner of administering this sacrament correctly, so that in case of necessity, when a priest cannot be called, they will know how to proceed. The pastor is thus obligated not only to teach the proper manner of administering the sacrament, but also to examine the faithful on their knowledge concerning this namely, whether they know the prescribed matter, form, and intention to be had. This instruction is to be given to Catholics only as is clear from the word *fideles,* as used in the canon. However, because of the importance of receiving this sacrament, well-disposed non-Catholics should also be instructed, especially nurses and doctors, wherever this is possible; for it may be said that usually such nurses and doctors will dutifully coöperate in respecting and fulfilling the teachings of the Church in this matter as reflected in the wishes of the parents.

Canon 770: Infantes quamprimum baptizentur; et parochi ac concionatores frequenter fideles de hac gravi obligatione commoneant.

[78] Canon 1395, § 1.

[79] Canon 469; Augustine, *Commentary,* VI, 642.

[80] Conc. Trid., sess. VI, *de Bapt.,* cap. 4.

Because of the necessity of Baptism, infants are to be baptized as soon as possible. If the infant is in danger of death, Baptism is to be administered immediately. However, if the infant is in good health, it is a mooted point just what lapse of time in deferring its baptism would constitute matter for grave sin. Some authors are of the opinion that a serious violation of the law is occasioned only when the delay has been protracted for about a month,[81] but the more common teaching of theologians and canonists supports the view that a mortal sin arises through a delay of ten or eleven days,[82] if no just cause excuses.

> **Canon 1018: Parochus ne omittat populum prudenter erudire de matrimonii sacramento ejusque impedimentis.**

This canon defines the pastor's obligation to instruct the people on the Church's teaching as it concerns the sacrament of Matrimony as well as its impediments. From the words *ne omittat*, it is clear that the obligation of giving these instructions is a serious one. The people must be taught the sacramental nature of the matrimonial contract, and especially should they be given to understand that a marriage contracted without the form prescribed by the Church is null and void. Moreover, they should be instructed summarily in regard to the necessary conditions of consent for a valid contract, at least concerning the liberty of action that is required. Finally, they must be given a clear understanding of the impediments to marriage, particularly those which occur more frequently, such as mixed and disparate marriages, as well as a brief description of the obligations and duties proper to the married life. The canon prescribes that these instructions should be given prudently, so as not to offend the listeners in those elements which might become the occasion of harm through scandal and suggestion rather than accomplish the good effects which are desired.[83]

[81] Lehmkuhl, *Theol. Moralis,* II, p. 60; Sabetti-Barrett, *Theol. Moralis,* p. 584.

[82] Aertnys-Damen, *Theologia Moralis,* II, 45.

cause excuses.

[83] Vermeersch-Creusen, *Epitome,* II, 176.

In as far as possible and in correspondence to the general and particular needs of the parishioners this instruction is to be offered both publicly and privately.[84] This rule regarding the instruction on the impediments in general receives full corroboration from the attitude of the Holy See concerning the need of public and private instruction in reference to the impediments of disparity of cult and mixed religion in particular. The Third Council of Baltimore, in order to reduce the number of mixed and disparate marriages to a minimum, enacted specific legislation:

> . . . Ad hunc autem finem assequendum maxime conducit: 1° frequens parochorum instructio qua fideles edoceantur de Ecclesiae prohibitione mixtorum matrimoniorum. 2° Praxis uniformis eorumdem parochorum in casibus occurrentibus impediendi totis viribus, hortationibus, suasionibus, necnon increpationibus ne hujusmodi conjugia ineantur. 3° Examen accuratum de canonicis et gravibus causis quae requiruntur pro dispensatione super hoc mixtae communionis impedimento concedenda. 4° Post celebratas autem mixtas nuptias, parochi gravi conscientiae onere se gravari sciant invigilandi ut promissae a conjugibus conditiones observentur et effectum sortiantur.[85]

In addition, the pastor should warn the young people of his parish that it is sinful to wish to contract a mixed marriage on account of mutual love without any grave cause as is required by the Church in granting a dispensation from the laws established. Parents must be admonished to be vigilant lest their children cultivate friendships that might lead to mixed marriage. While the pastor should use due prudence and charity in speaking of these impediments, he should, nevertheless, explain the complete doctrine of the Church, without being conciliatory either from human respect of from any false principle of tolerance. Besides preaching sermons which deal directly with this subject, he should emphasize it also when giving instructions on other topics, such as dangers to the Faith, the duties of parents,

[84] "Edocendi denique fideles qua publicis catechesibus, qua privatis instructionibus circa constantem hac in re Ecclesiae doctrinam, ne unquam eos capiat oblivio canonum mixta connubia detestantium." S. C. S. Off., Instr. (Ad omnes Ep. Ritus Orient.), Dec. 12, 1888, n. 11—*Fontes*, n. 1112.

[85] *Conc. Plen. Balt.*, III, n. 133.

the choice of a state of life, and kindred subjects, all of which may suggest or even invite the expression of some wholesome thought or the mention of relevant detail about the responsibilities of wedded life and the need of a holy preparation for it.[86]

Privately, the pastor should make use of those opportunities that are presented, as for instance on the occasion of the parish census, to teach both parents and children the dangers and evils associated with such marriages. Likewise, when he observes that one of his parishioners is maintaining a friendship which might lead to such a marriage, he should counsel him either personally or through his parents of the consequences.[87]

Canon 1033: Ne omittat parochus, secundum diversam personarum conditionem, sponsos docere sanctitatem sacramenti matrimonii, mutuas coniugum obligationes et obligationes parentum erga prolem; eosdemque vehementer adhortetur ut ante matrimonii celebrationem sua peccata diligenter confiteantur, et sanctissimam Eucharistiam pie recipiant.

The instruction required by this canon refers to that which is given by the proper pastor or his assistant to the parties previous to marriage. As such it is not to be confused with the examination required to prove the absence of impediments and the presence of the necessary knowledge of the truths of Faith.[88] The pastor is obligated *sub gravi* to give these instructions when it is certain that the contracting parties have not been previously instructed. In the latter instance the obligation is only a light one, and the instructions may be omitted for a just cause if they cannot be conveniently given.[89] The thoroughness of this instruction is to be determined by

[86] Ter Haar, *De Matrimoniis Mixtis Eorumque Remediis*, pp. 73, 74.

[87] "Hinc oportet animarum curatores monere, ut gregi suo solertes invigilando, simul ac compererint adesse iuvenes vel virgines coniugale foedus cum heterodoxis inire volentes, ipsos eorumque parentes salutaribus imbuant doctrinis, nihilque omittant, quo eos a transgrediendis Dei et Ecclesiae mandatis avertant." S. C. S. Off., instr. (Ad omnes Ep. Ritus Orient.), Dec. 12, 1888, n. 11—*Fontes*, n. 1112.

[88] Canon 1020, § 2.

[89] Cappello, *De Sacramentis*, III (*De Matrimonio*), 220.

the pastor. If it is clear that the parties to marriage are well aware of their duties, it will be enough to exhort and admonish them to fulfill them faithfully as becomes a Christian husband and wife. It is also recommended that the parties be instructed prudently. Moreover, these instructions ought to be given outside of the confessional.[90] The practice of instructing the parties in the confessional, apart from the fact that it is not mentioned by the canon, does not seem to be conformable to the juridic nature of Penance and is rather permitted in view of circumstances which in a given case allow a deviation from the normal method of procedure.[91]

In this instruction, the pastor is briefly to explain the great dignity of the sacrament as instituted by Christ, and its inseparability from the matrimonial contract.[92] The ends for which this sacrament was instituted are to be indicated, namely, the propagation of the human race, a means of insuring marital chastity, and the mutual assistance husband and wife are to give each other in the contingencies of life through the practice of the virtues of patience, kindness, and loyalty.[93] The manner in which the parties should prepare themselves for the reception of this sacrament should be indicated; and, if a civil act is required by law, they should be told with what intention they are to fulfill this requirement.[94] The pastor should also point out the mutual fidelity which they must observe toward each other as well as their mutual conjugal rights and duties.[95] The husband is to be informed in a general way concerning his rights and duties as head of the family, namely, that it is his responsibility to govern the home, to maintain domestic discipline, and provide for the temporal welfare; the wife is to be admonished of the reverence which she is to show toward her husband and the obedience due him in all things which are not opposed to Christian piety, as well as diligently to care for the home.[96] The obligation of parents towards their children,

[90] Payen, *De Matrimonio,* I, 336; Cappello, *op. cit.,* 219.

[91] Gasparri, *De Matrimonio,* I, n. 195.

[92] Canon 1012.

[93] Canon 1013.

[94] Aertnys-Damen, *Theologia Moralis,* II, 466.

[95] Canon 1111.

[96] Payen, *De Matrimonio,* I, 367, 368; Aertnys-Damen, *Theologia Moralis,* II, 580; Cappello, *De Sacramentis,* III, 219.

especially in regard to their religious education, is also to be explained. Finally, in order that the contracting parties may worthily receive this sacrament of Matrimony and thereby gain the more abundant graces to aid them in fulfilling their duties in a Christian manner, the pastor should earnestly exhort them to receive the sacraments of Penance and the Holy Eucharist. From the wording of the canon it is clear that confession is not required, either by the divine or by the ecclesiastical law.[97] *Per accidens,* however, confession would be necessary in the case of a public sinner, who desires to contract marriage in the place where he is known as such, in order to remove scandal; but, if such a one should refuse to go to confession, marriage cannot be simply denied. A grave cause is required for the pastor to assist at this marriage, however, and if possible, he should consult the local ordinary.[98] Similarly, confession would be required in the instance when the grant of a necessary dispensation from an impediment could not otherwise be given except in the sacramental forum. The phrase *ante matrimonii celebrationem* refers rather to confession only, especially since it is recommended that the parties receive Holy Communion during the Nuptial Mass. However, this is by no means necessary since the couple to be married may receive these sacraments the day previous to the marriage.[99]

Canon 1273: Qui in religiosam fidelium institutionem incumbunt, nihil omittant ut pietatem erga sanctissimam Eucharistiam in eorum animis excitent, eosque praesertim hortentur ut, non modo diebus dominicis et festis de praecepto, sed etiam diebus ferialibus intra hebdomadam, frequenter, quantum fieri potest, Missae sacrificio assistant et sanctissimum Sacramentum visitent.

Little need be said to clarify the meaning of this canon. Its basis

[97] The reference here is to the universal law of the Church. In case it should be commanded by particular law, this would have to be understood in the wide sense, because, strictly speaking, such a requirement cannot be given as it would be opposed to the law of the Code.—Cappello, *op. cit.*, III, 221, 222.

[98] Canon 1066.

[99] Payen, *op. cit.*, I, 370, 371; Gasparri, *De Matrimonio,* I, n. 243.

is in the fact that our Blessed Lord is to be adored and praised in His real presence in the sacrament of the Most Holy Eucharist, the center around which the entire Christian life revolves. Simply stated, this law is a grievous precept that pastors and others having the care of souls must excite in the hearts of the faithful a vivid consciousness of this real presence of the Eucharistic Lord, which is to be manifested by attendance at daily Mass as well as by frequent visits to the Blessed Sacrament:

> "Sicut in ipso fidei intellectu, ita in exhibitione caritatis erga Christum crescit vera Ecclesia, Ejus sponsa." [100]

Indeed, the certain barometer, so to speak, that the pastor has in measuring how successful his efforts have been in fulfilling the law of catechetical instruction is the devotion that his parishioners have cultivated towards the Blessed Sacrament.

[100] Vermeersch-Creusen, *Epitome,* II, 371.

CHAPTER V

THE OBLIGATION OF PARENTS AND SPONSORS

Article 1. A Summary of the Relations Between the Family, the State, and the Church

The catechetical program of ecclesiastical legislation as outlined in the preceding chapters in reality determines the means which parents and those who hold their place are to make use of in the education of their children in the truths of Christianity. It is necessary, therefore, as a preliminary to the interpretation of the canonical obligations of parents in this matter, to explain in a brief manner the Church's right to impose these. For in the education of the child, three social units have correlative rights, namely the family, the Church, and the State. That the primary right to education belongs to the family is vindicated by the natural law: for the father of the child is not only the principle of generation but also of education, discipline, and everything that bears upon the perfection of human life.[1] The reason for this is that nature intends not only the mere generation of offspring, but also their development to the perfection of manhood.[2] Because of the fact that infants are neither able to conserve their own life or by their own abilities to arrive at the full status of man, this obligation resides in the parents anterior to any other agency. The reason for this is that by nature the child is something of the father and as a consequence is under the father's care before he has reached the complete use of reason. Therefore, it would be contrary to the inviolable natural right of the parents if the child, before attaining the use of reason, were removed from their care, or if any dispositions were made concerning the child against their will.[3] This parental right is not absolute, however, but is con-

[1] *Summa Theol.*, II-IIa, q. 102, a. 1.

[2] *Summa Theol. Suppl.*, III, q. 41, a. 1.

[3] *Summa Theol.*, II-IIa, q. 10, a. 12.

ditioned by God's plan—by His law and the divinely established order.

By reason of the authority given to it by God to promote the common welfare of society, the State also has certain rights and duties in the field of education. It has the right to exact from its citizens a knowledge of their civil and political duties, and in view of the common good, a certain standard of physical, intellectual, and moral culture. To insure the attainment and maintenance of this standard, the State has the corresponding duty to supplement the insufficient resources of the family and to protect the rights of the child when its parents fail to do so because of physical or moral impediments. While the State has a rightful place in education, it nevertheless needs to be noted that it has the duty at all times to respect and protect not only the rights of the family (because they are prior by nature), but also to recognize the rights of the Church and to assist in the work which she, by reason of her divine foundation, is to accomplish.[4] For man is destined to a supernatural end which his education must equip him to attain. It is for this reason that the Church is authorized to teach. This supernatural right is moreover in harmony with, but not subordinate to, the natural right of the family or the State. It is in harmony because the supernatural order not only does not destroy the natural order to which the rights of the family and the State owe their origin, but elevates and perfects it, affording aid to these two agencies according to the respective nature and dignity of each. It is not subordinate because the Church enjoys jurisdiction in a sphere that is exclusively her own, namely the supernatural order. This right of the Church is based on two supernatural titles: "The first title is based upon the express mission and supreme authority to teach given her by her divine founder" and the second is "the *supernatural motherhood* which belongs to the Church as the spotless Bride of Christ. In virtue of this the Church begets, nourishes, and rears all souls in respect to their supernatural life of grace through her Sacraments and her teaching."[5]

In recognition, therefore, of the mutual coöperation that is to

[4] Pius XI, litt. encycl., *Divini illius magistri,* Dec. 31, 1929—*AAS,* XXII (1929), 49ss.

[5] Pius XI, *loc. cit.*

exist between these agencies, the Church has thus defined the obligation which parents have to procure the proper education of their children:

> **Canon 1113: Parentes gravissima obligatione tenentur prolis educationem tum religiosam et moralem, tum physicam et civilem pro viribus curandi, et etiam temporali eorum bono providendi.**

This canon indicates the characteristics, so to speak, of the education which parents must be solicitous to procure for the child, not only by their own personal influence, but also by making use of the means which the State and the Church have provided. Proper care must be taken for the child's physical education, that is, its life, food, and material status. Moreover, every effort must be made to see to it that the child becomes a worthy member of the political society in which it has been born. Finally, parents must make ample provision for the proper religious and moral education of their offspring, on which the eternal happiness or punishment of the child to a large extent depends.[6] It is primarily with this religious and moral education that the Church is concerned in her legislation respecting catechetical instruction.

Article 2. The Extent of the Obligation of Parents and Those Who Hold the Place of Parents

By parents are meant those who are such by reason of the natural generation of the child and not by reason of marriage. Hence parents of illegitimate and spurious children are obliged to provide for the religious and moral instruction of these. In case the child's parents are dead, or otherwise incapacitated, this obligation devolves *per se* on the ascendants, that is, the grandfather and grandmother, and in their absence, on the lawfully constituted guardians. Likewise, institutions such as orphan asylums to which a child may be committed are bound to care for its religious training. This will in-

[6] Aertnys-Damen, *Theologia Moralis,* III, 366-371; Payen, *De Matrimonio,* II, 459-470.

clude the following duties, concerning which pastors and preachers are frequently to remind the people.[7]

In the first place, parents should seek to have their children baptized as soon as possible after birth.[8] Also in the case of a miscarriage, of the issue of an abortive fetus, or of the emergence of a fetal deformity or freakish living growth baptism is to be administered, either absolutely or conditionally as attendant conditions will justify or demand.[9] The lapse of time within which baptism must be conferred has already been discussed.[10] Parents who deliberately and knowingly allow their children to be baptized by non-Catholic ministers incur *ipso facto* an excommunication, the absolution of which is reserved to the ordinary of the place.[11]

After baptism, parents are to see to it that the gift of Faith is nourished and strengthened as the child advances in age.[12] This is accomplished by Christian education which is rooted in the home and continues in the parish classes and the parochial schools. The first and most far-reaching obligation imposed on parents is that of giving good example, that is, of living according to the Christian principles which are to be inculcated in the life of the child. The necessity of this example on the part of parents has its basis in the child's highly developed power of imitation. In addition, it seems that there are also certain other minimum requirements for parents. These include among others the giving of simple instructions which should begin early in the life of the child since it is capable of learning much about Christianity during pre-school years. Pedagogical experiments have proved that a child of three years is capable of

[7] Canons 770, 467, § 2, 1348.

[8] Canon 770.

[9] Canons 747 and 749.

[10] *Cf. Supra*, p. 103.

[11] Canon 2319, § 1, 3°: Parents who would commit this offense are likewise suspected of heresy (Canon 2319, § 2) and subject to the penalties of Canon 2315.

[12] Quisquis unum ex huiusmodi pueris receperit, in nomine meo, me recipit." —Mark ix. 36.

"Filii tibi sunt? Erudi illos, et curva illos a pueritia illorum."—Eccl. vii. 25.

"Adolescens juxta viam suam, etiam cum senuerit, non recedet ab ea."—Proverbs xxii. 6.

grasping some realization of God as the Creator, of Heaven as the place of reward for the good, and in addition certain moral ideas, as for instance, obedience and honesty. Likewise it is capable of learning some of the more simple prayers. The presence in the home of pictures of our Lord, of His Blessed Mother, and of the Saints, assist in impressing upon the mind of the child strong and fundamental religious ideas. The deep impressions that these earliest influences make afford ample corroboration of the opinion that parents are obliged, according to their ability, to provide for such training. When the child has attained the use of reason, parents are either to continue to teach the child its catechism, or to employ a private tutor to do so, or to use the means afforded by the parish (*i. e.*, the parochial school or parish classes) or to send the child to some other Catholic school. This is implied by the word *curandi* as used to define the extent of parental obligations:

> **Canon 1335: . . . parentes aliique qui parentum locum tenent . . . obligatione adstringuntur curandi ut omnes sibi subjecti . . . catechetica institutione erudiantur.**

Relative to the parish classes (which are of primary concern here), parents are required to observe the regulations which outline the program of religious instruction. In brief, they will first send their children to the general classes, and likewise at the proper time to the classes preparatory to the reception of the sacraments of Penance, Confirmation, and Holy Eucharist; finally they will see to it that their children attend the advanced classes. Since these are conducted in parishes where there are no parochial schools and the children as a consequence attend the public (neutral or mixed) schools, parents must be particularly alert in the fulfillment of their duty. For such a school system constitutes in itself a danger to the Faith of the child as has been indicated by Pope Pius XI:

> From this it follows that the so-called "neutral" or "lay" school, from which religion is excluded, is contrary to the fundamental principles of education. Such a school moreover cannot exist in practice; it is bound to become irreligious.[13]

[13] Litt. encycl., *Divini illius magistri*—*AAS*, XXII (1929).

It is evident, therefore, how serious the obligation of parents is to take care that their children receive the necessary instruction both in faith and morals in the parish classes. They must see to it that the danger of perversion is removed by opportune remedies and precautionary measures. This will include vigilance lest anything of a perversive nature is taught in the school or lest too great a familiarity might be engendered with those from whom a danger of such perversion might result.

The ordinary of the place has it within his power to insure the proper fulfillment of parental responsibilities. In the first place, it is left to his judgment to determine whether or not a sufficient cause is present to permit attendance at public schools.[14] While no punishments are established by the common law for parents who neglect to send their children to the parish classes, it is within the ordinary's power [15] to determine suitable penalties (*e. g.*, personal interdict) for parents who would be contumacious in this matter. In such instances, however, care must be taken that sufficient warning is given concerning such punishments.[16] In the internal forum, parents who would be gravely negligent in the proper religious training of their children are to be denied sacramental absolution.[17] It may also be pointed out here that, according to the common law, parents who deliberately (*i. e.*, with a knowledge of the law and its punishment) send their children to a school to be educated in a non-Catholic religion incur *ipso facto* excommunication, the absolution of which is reserved to the ordinary.[18] To incur this censure, they must know that such a school not only does not attempt to observe neutrality in religious matters, but also *ex professo* teaches heretical doctrines.

In the preparation of children for first Communion, parents have certain rights and obligations, based on the requirement that the

[14] Canon 1374; S. C. S. Off., instr. (Ad Episcopos Stat. Foed. Amer. Sept.), Nov. 24, 1875—*Acta et Decreta Concilii Plenarii Baltimorensis Tertii*, pp. 279-282.

[15] Canon 2220.

[16] Canons 2221 and 2201, § 1; also Canon 2233, § 2.

[17] Aertnys-Damen, *Theologia Moralis*, II, 357.

[18] Canon 2319, § 1, 4°; by reason of paragraph two of this same canon, such parents are also suspected of heresy.

candidates know the principal mysteries of Faith and understand Who is received in Communion.[19] Lest any abuse should arise through neglect, pastors are obliged to give proper instruction to the children so that they approach the Communion table with the proper dispositions both of mind and of heart.[20] Judgment concerning these dispositions belongs to the parents and to the confessor in coöperation with the pastor.[21] Strictly speaking, however, it does not seem necessary for parents to notify the pastor concerning their children's readiness to be admitted to first Communion, neither does the pastor have the right of insisting that children attend the preparatory classes in their proper parish.[22] However, if he should have reason to doubt the mental development of any child, or its moral dispositions, or its preparatory training, he must have such a one submit to an examination to determine its fitness.[23] Because of the right of the parents in this matter, Vermeersch is of the opinion that a pastor may not oblige the candidates as a group to submit to an examination as a condition for admittance to the reception of first Communion.[24] This opinion explains the relationship between parents and the pastor in this matter; it also indicates how the canonical regulations respect the prior right of the parents and recognize their competence to estimate, because of the daily contact with the children, the required dispositions, in which they are also assisted by the confessor.

Article 3. Obligation of Employers

Canon 1335: . . . heri quoque . . . obligatione adstringuntur curandi ut omnes sibi subiecti vel commendati catechetica institutione erudiantur.

In using the word *heri* (owner, master), those only are included who employ domestic servants in their household. They are obliged

19 S. C. de Sacr., decr., *Quam singulari,* Aug. 8, 1910—*Fontes,* n. 2103.

20 Canon 1330, 2°.

21 Canon 854, § 4.

22 DeMeester, *Juris Canonici et Juris Canonici-civilis Compendium,* II, 277; Ayrinhac, *Legislation on the Sacraments,* p. 166.

23 Canon 854, § 5.

24 *Epitome,* II, 82.

both in justice and in charity to provide for their employees ample opportunity for proper training in the knowledge and practice of their religion. This obligation is twofold, namely, it is required that no obstacle be placed to prevent these employees from the fulfillment of their religious duties, and that they attend or receive instruction as their condition demands.[25] "If any man," says St. Paul, "have not the care of his own and especially of those of his house, he hath denied the faith and is worse than an infidel." [26]

Article 4. Obligation of Sponsors

Canon 1335: . . . Patrini obligatione adstringuntur curandi ut omnes sibi subiecti vel commendati catechetica institutione erudiantur.

Canon 769: Patrinorum est, ex suscepto munere, spiritualem filium perpetuo sibi commendatum habere, atque in iis quae ad christianae vitae institutionem spectant, curare diligenter ut ille talem in tota vita se praebeat, qualem futurum esse sollemni caeremonia spoponderunt.

Canon 797: Etiam ex valida confirmatione oritur inter confirmatum et patrinum cognatio spiritualis, ex qua patrinus obligatione tenetur confirmatum perpetuo sibi commendatum habendi eiusque christianem educationem curandi.

By these laws the Church has enlarged the family circle to include also the godparents in order that the child might be given greater security against misfortunes that might result from the loss or neglect of the parents. The importance of this office of godparents is indicated by the canonical effects which, by reason of ecclesiastical law arise from the spiritual relationship contracted by sponsor and child.[27]

Whenever a child's Christian education has not been or cannot be supplied by its parents or by those who share their primary re-

[25] Benedict XIV, litt. encycl., *Cum Religiosis,* June 26, 1754—*Fontes,* n. 429.
[26] 1 Tim. v. 8.
[27] Canons 768 and 797.

sponsibilities in this matter, then it becomes the direct duty of the sponsor to instruct the child and likewise to provide for its attendance at the catechetical classes. In a subordinate way sponsors should exercise a constant vigilance over their spiritual children. In as much as a sponsor usually enjoys a friendly contact with the home life of the child, he becomes coadjutor, as it were, to the pastor of the parish in remedying whatever neglect parents may show. The duties of a sponsor become particularly pressing when circumstances in a given case betray a serious neglect on the part of the parents.[28]

[28] *The Catechism of the Council of Trent* (tr. by J. Donovan), pp. 122, 123.

SUPPLEMENT I

List of Indulgences

In order to show the importance which the Church attaches to the ministry of catechetics, and to encourage as many as possible to devote their efforts to this work, the Holy See has granted many indulgences. These have been granted for the faithful in general and for the members of both the Confraternity of Christian Doctrine and the Catholic Instruction League. The following list is in harmony with the most recent revisions made by the Holy See:

A. For the Faithful in General

Pope Pius XI [1] has granted the following indulgences to all the faithful (whether they are members of the Confraternity of Christian Doctrine or not) who either teach or study Christian doctrine at least twice during the month for a period of not less than twenty minutes. Any one who thus performs this work may, twice during the month on any day chosen, gain:

(a) A *plenary* indulgence provided that he, being truly penitent, receives the sacraments of Penance and Holy Eucharist, and in addition makes a visit to a church or public oratory and there recites some prayers for the intention of the Holy Father.[2]

(b) A *partial* indulgence—which presupposes at least contriteness of heart—may be gained not only twice during the month (like the plenary indulgence) but as often as Christian doctrine has been

[1] Pius XI, *litt.*, March 12, 1930—*AAS*, XXII (1930), 343. With this concession the indulgences granted by Paul V (1605-1621) and Clement XII (1730-1740) have been expressly abrogated.

[2] By a visit to a church or public oratory is meant going to the same at least with some general or implicit intention of honoring God in Himself or in His saints. For the intention of the Holy Father, it is sufficient to say one *Pater, Ave,* and *Gloria,* although any other prayers, according to Canon 934, § 1, may be recited.—S. Poenit. Ap., *decl.*, Sept. 20, 1933—*AAS*, XXV (1933), 446.

taught or studied during the time prescribed (*i.e.*, at least twenty minutes).

Likewise, Pius IX, on July 18, 1877, granted:

(c) *Partial* indulgences to be gained on feasts of the Blessed Virgin by all the faithful who are wont to assemble in schools and churches to learn Christian Doctrine—seven years for those who go to confession and receive Holy Communion, and three years for those who go to confession only. In accordance with canon 931, § 2, such a prescribed confession is to be made at any time within the octave immediately preceding the day on which the indulgence is to be gained, while Holy Communion must be received either on the feast day or its vigil.[3]

B. For Members of the Confraternity of Christian Doctrine

Pope Pius X[4] fixed definitely the list of indulgences and privileges that could be gained by members of the Confraternity only. This list, in harmony with recent decrees of the Sacred Penitentiary, includes:

I. A *plenary* indulgence to be gained under the usual conditions of receiving the sacraments of Penance and Holy Eucharist, and praying for the intention of the Holy Father:

(1) By members on the day of their reception into the Confraternity.

(2) By each member on the principal feasts of the local Confraternity.

(3) By each member on the following feasts: Easter, Christmas, Pentecost, Epiphany, Ascension, Circumcision, Assumption, and The Immaculate Conception of the Blessed Virgin Mary; feast of Our Lady of Seven Sorrows (January 14th—titular feast of the Church of Santa Maria del Pianto in Rome, the center of the Archconfra-

[3] Beringer-Steinen, *Die Ablässe*, I, n. 802.

[4] "Sanctissimus D. N. benignc approbare dignatus est supra relatum summarium, simulque mandavit, tantummodo Indulgentiis et Privilegiis ibi inscriptis in posterum memoratam Archi-confraternitatem frui posse. Contrariis quibuscumque non obstantibus." S. C. S. Off., Decr., June 6, 1912—*AAS*, IV (1912), 587, 588.

ternity); feasts of St. Joseph (March 19th), Sts. Peter and Paul (June 29th), All Saints, St. Charles Borromeo (November 4th), St. Joseph Calasanctius (August 27th) and St. Robert Bellarmine (May 13th).[5]

(4) By each member who, at the hour of death, having confessed and received Holy Communion, or in as far as he was unable to do this, having devoutly invoked the Name of Jesus, orally if possible, otherwise interiorly, shall patiently accept death as the wages of sin.

II. The indulgences of the *Roman Stations.*[6] The indulgences, granted by Pope Pius X, have been confirmed by the Sacred Penitentiary.[7] Independent of any consideration of the Confraternity of Christian Doctrine, the Sacred Penitentiary drew up a list of these indulgences and the manner of gaining them:

(1) A *plenary* indulgence to those, who having confessed and received Holy Communion, on the day of a Station devoutly visit the station church and assist at the functions, morning or evening, according to the local custom or the instructions of the Pope.

(2) A *plenary* indulgence (under the usual conditions to those who visit the station church and in the absence of any public service, there recite five *Paters, Aves* and *Glorias* before the Blessed Sacrament, three *Paters, Aves,* and *Glorias* before any relics displayed for veneration, and at least one *Pater, Ave,* and *Gloria* for the intention of the Holy Father.

(3) A *partial* indulgence of ten years may be gained by visiting the station church and reciting the above listed prayers.[8]

When Pius X extended the privilege of gaining these indulgences

[5] S. Poenit. Ap., decr., March 2, 1932—*AAS,* XXIV (1932), 249.

[6] On certain days, the Pope was accustomed to offer the Sacrifice of the Mass at a certain church in the city of Rome. These churches have been designated as station churches, and are noted in the Roman Missal.

[7] ". . . Peculiaria ejusmodi indulta ita in posterum intelligenda esse ut valeant adscripti indulgentias stationales in ecclesiis etiam non stationalibus, ceteris ad rem clausulis et praescriptionibus ad unguem servatis, adipisci tum tantum cum nullae in loco ecclesiae stationales inveniantur." S. Poenit. Ap., Feb. 25, 1933—*AAS,* XXV (1933), 72.

[8] S. Poenit. Ap., April 12, 1932—*AAS,* XXIV (1932), 248, 249.

to members of the Confraternity of Christian Doctrine,[9] the only requirements seemed to be the teaching, supervision, or attendance at the catechetical classes under the usual conditions of confession and Communion, with the former being substituted for the visit to the church and the recitation of the prescribed prayers. However, the Sacred Penitentiary, in renewing this privilege of the Station indulgences for those pious associations who had previously obtained such, now requires the conditions to be fulfilled as given above, namely, the visit to the church and the recitation of the prescribed prayers. So that for members of the Confraternity of Christian Doctrine, this will be necessary in addition to teaching, supervising, or attending classes of religious instruction.

III. *Partial indulgences:*

(1) Ten years to members who go into rural districts to teach catechism.

(2) Seven years and seven quarantines if the members fulfill the usual conditions (confession, Communion, and prayers according to the intention of the Holy Father) on the day and in the place where the Confraternity is being erected; the same indulgence once a month when the sacraments are received.

(3) Seven years to priest members who give instruction in a church or oratory of the Confraternity.

(4) Seven years to members who bring men, women, and children to religious instruction.

(5) Seven years to members if they accompany the Blessed Sacrament when it is borne to the sick.

(6) Three years to those members who attend the funeral of a deceased member or accompany the body to the cemetery, and pray for the repose of his soul.

(7) Two hundred days for those who visit sick members; two hundred days for those who attend the pious exercises, reunions, or processions of the Confraternity, held with the approval of the ordinary of the place; two hundred days to members who provide for children, servants, and others in their care to attend the instruction classes.

[9] June 6, 1912—*AAS,* IV (1912), 587, 588.

(8) One hundred days for those, who publicly or privately, explain the catechism on other than feast days.[10]

IV. Privileges:

(1) All priests who were members of the Confraternity *before* April 1, 1933 have the personal privilege of the privileged altar four days of the week when they offer Mass for the soul of any of the faithful departed.[11] Clerics, however, who were enrolled in the Confraternity before April 1, 1933, but were not as yet ordained to the priesthood, do not enjoy this privilege.[12]

(2) When a Mass is offered by any priest at any altar for the soul of a deceased member of the Confraternity, it has the same efficacy as Mass celebrated at a privileged altar.[13]

C. For members of the Catholic Instruction League

Pope Pius XI, in his brief of the fifth of August, 1925, granted the following indulgences to members of the Catholic Instruction League:

(1) A *plenary* indulgence to all members on the day of joining this Pious Union on condition that being truly penitent and having confessed their sins, they shall have received Holy Communion.

(2) A *plenary* indulgence to all members to be gained at the hour of death, provided that, being truly penitent, they shall have confessed their sins and received Holy Communion, or in as far as they were unable to do this, shall have devoutly invoked the Name

[10] In virtue of Canon 930, all these indulgences, with the exception of that to be gained at the hour of death, are applicable to the souls in Purgatory.

[11] In virtue of the decree of the Sacred Penitentiary of March 20, 1933 (*AAS,* XXV [1933], 170, 171), the Confraternity can no longer grant this privilege, although the faculty to do so has not been abrogated. Therefore, priests who enrolled as members before April 1, 1933, have not lost this privilege.—*Periodica,* XXII (1933), 107; *AER,* LXXXIX (1933), 182.

[12] S. Poenit. Ap., *Dubia super decreto "Consilium suum persequens,"* March 2, 1937, ad I—*AAS,* XXIX (1937), 57.

[13] This privilege has not been revoked for the above-mentioned decree speaks only of the faculty which pious associations possess to grant this privilege to *priest-members*. In this instance, however, the reference is to a privilege granted to every priest, not because he is a member, but rather because he offers Mass for the intention of some deceased member.

of Jesus, orally if they were able, otherwise interiorly, and shall patiently accept death as the wages of sin.

(3) A *plenary* indulgence to all members, under the usual conditions, who shall have confessed and communicated on the Feasts of the Blessed Virgin Mary, Mediatrix of all Graces (May 31st), of St. Joseph, of the Holy Innocents, and of St. Agnes (January 21st), provided that once a week for at least four months they shall have taught Christian doctrine.

(4) A *plenary* indulgence to all of the boys and girls who attend the classes on the occasion of their first Holy Communion, and to the catechists who receive Communion with the children, under the usual conditions.

(5) A *partial* indulgence of seven years, to be gained once a month, to members, if they shall have taught Christian doctrine to the children, at least twice in a month.[14]

[14] Bouscaren, *The Canon Law Digest (Cumulative Supplement, 1935-1936)*, pp. 68, 69.

SUPPLEMENT II

RELIGIOUS INSTRUCTION TO PUBLIC SCHOOL PUPILS UNDER AMERICAN CIVIL LAW

The present-day legal prohibitions of religious instruction in the public-school system of the United States has been largely a result of the development of the system itself. In its early beginnings in the New England Colonies, one of the primary functions of the school was to impart religious instruction. And not only did such a practice have the approval of the local town governments, but the latter also gave financial assistance to the school. Even the approbation of teachers by the ministers was required by law in some instances.[1] With the growth of the colonies and the spread of different religious groups, difficulties arose out of such provisions, with the result that private schools were organized, supported either by religious groups, charitable donations, or secular organizations, which continued to provide a religious education. The post-Revolutionary period witnessed no great development of the public school system. With its introduction, however, in the period preceding the Civil War [2] religious instruction continued to be given. However, acrimonious differences in religious belief, centralization of school control, and support from public funds made the teaching of religion difficult. The development of the idea of universal education in one school system combined with the firmly established constitutional principle of religious liberty led to its gradual elimination. The movement crystallized after the Civil War during the presidency of Grant, who thus gave expression in an address delivered at Des Moines, Iowa, on September 29, 1875: "Resolve that neither the state nor the nation, nor both combined, shall support institutions

[1] Riley, *Catholicism in New England to 1788* (Washington, 1936), pp. 256-259.

[2] Monroe, *A Brief Course in the History of Education*, p. 392; McCormick, *History of Education*, pp. 382, 383.

of learning other than those sufficient to afford every child growing up in the land the opportunity of a good common school education, unmixed with sectarian, pagan or atheistical dogmas. Leave the matter of religion to the family altar, the church, and the private school, supported entirely by private contributions." [3] In the same year, an amendment to the United States Constitution was recommended which prohibited the teaching of religion and public support for any religious sect. This was defeated in the Senate on August 14, 1876.[4]

However, in order to eliminate any future difficulties that might arise, religious instruction of a sectarian nature has been made illegal in many States. This has been done in two ways:

(a) By a Federal compact imposed on new States admitted to the Union since 1876. This consists in the provision, as a requirement for admission, for a school system which shall be open to all children and free from sectarian control.

(b) By State constitutional provisions which prevent any sectarian control of the school system.[5]

The fact that the policy of education has thus crystallized accounts for the absence of such provisions in other States: "If there is any one thing which is well settled in the policies and purposes of the American people as a whole, it is the fixed and unalterable determination that there shall be an absolute and unequivocal separation of Church and State, and that our public school system, supported by the taxation of the property of all alike—Catholic, Protestant, Jew, Gentile, believer, and infidel—shall not be used directly or indirectly for religious instruction, and above all that it shall not be made an instrumentality of proselyting influence in favor of any religious organization, sect, creed, or belief." [6]

Despite this inevitable and rather negative solution of the problem, the fact remains that the common welfare of any society

[3] *Congressional Record,* Vol. 4, pt. 1, p. 175.

[4] *Congressional Record,* Vol. 4, pt. 1, p. 5595.

[5] Nebraska (1875), art. 8; Colorado (1876), art. 9, § 8; California (1879), art. 9, § 8; Montana (1889), art. 11, § 9; Idaho (1889), art. 9, § 6; South Dakota (1889), art. 8, § 16; Wyoming (1889), art. 7, § 12; Arizona, art. 11, § 7.

[6] Knowlton v. Baumhover (1918), 182 Iowa 691.

rests on the moral integrity of its citizenry, which can only be insured through sincere and thorough religious instruction. To provide for this, Bible reading, recitation of prayers, and singing of hymns has been rather weakly substituted in some States. That it has proved ineffectual is a matter of common conviction. Even in some instances, notably in Wisconsin, Illinois, and Nebraska, the courts have held that such reading of the Bible is sectarian instruction and public worship, and therefore contrary to the Constitution.

A more effective remedy has been attempted in some States. This consists in a statutory provision in the compulsory education clause of recognizing attendance at religious instruction as a just cause to excuse from school attendance. In these States, it would seem that the local ordinaries are to determine such provisions to be made use of in parishes where there are no parochial schools. Because this falls within the present discussion of catechetical instruction, these statutes are listed here:

> (a) *Minnesota:* "A child may be excused from attendance (at school) upon application of his parent, guardian, or other person having control of such child, to any member of the school board, truant officer, principal, or city superintendent, for the whole or any part of such period, by the school board of the district in which the child resides, upon its being shown to the satisfaction of such board:
>
> (3) That it is the wish of such parent, guardian, or other person having control of any child, that he attend for a period or periods not exceeding in the aggregate three hours in any week, a school for religious instruction, conducted and maintained by some church, or association of churches, or any Sunday school association incorporated under the laws of this state, or any auxiliary thereof, such a school to be conducted and maintained in a place other than a public school building, and in no event, in whole or in part of public expense; provided that no child shall be excused under this section while attending upon instruction, according to the ordinances of some church."[7]
>
> (b) *Iowa:* Children may be excused from school: "While attending religious services or receiving religious instruction."[8]

[7] *Mason's Minnesota Statutes* (1927), Vol. 1, § 3080.

[8] *Code of Iowa* (1935), § 4411.

(c) *Michigan:* "In the following cases children shall not be required to attend school:

(g) Confirmation class attendance; any child twelve (12) to fourteen (14) years of age, while in attendance at Confirmation classes conducted for a period not to exceed five (5) months in either of said years." [9]

(d) *South Dakota:* The County Superintendent shall have authority in all schools under his direct supervision and the Board of Education in all independent school districts employing and maintaining a superintendent for the schools of such independent district shall likewise have the power, to excuse a child from school attendance for following reasons:

(f) Provided further that a child may on application of his parent or guardian be excused from school for one hour per week for the purpose of taking and receiving religious instruction by some Church or Association of Churches or any Sunday School Association incorporated under the laws of the state or any auxiliary thereof; said time, when pertaining to schools in open country, may be used cumulatively each separate month, as local circumstances may require. The County Superintendent of Schools in common school districts and the Board of Education in consolidated and independent school districts shall decide at what hour scholars may thus be excused, and in no event shall such instruction be given in whole or in part at public expense.[10]

(e) *West Virginia:* Every person who has legal or actual charge of a child or children not less than seven nor more than fourteen years of age shall cause such child or children each year to attend a free day school for the full school term of the district or independent district in which such person resides: *Provided, however,* that such person shall be exempt from the foregoing requirement for any of the following causes:

(h) Observance of regular church ordinances.[11]

(f) *Oregon:* Any child attending the public school, on application of his guardian or either of his parents, may be excused from school for a period or periods not exceeding

[9] *The Compiled Laws of the State of Michigan* (1929), Vol. 2, § 7527.

[10] *South Dakota Compiled Laws* (1929), § 7642.

[11] *Official Code of West Virginia* (1931), Chap. 18, Art. 8, Sec. 1.

> one hundred and twenty (120) minutes in any week to attend weekday schools giving instruction in religion.[12]
>
> (g) *Illinois:* Every person having custody or control of any child between the ages of 7 and 16 years, shall annually cause such child to attend some public or private school for the entire time during which the public school in that district wherein the pupil resides is in session. Provided that in the following cases children shall not be required to attend the public schools:
>
> (d) Any child over 12 and under 14 years of age during the hours while in attendance at confirmation classes.[13]

While only seven States have provided by statute to permit attendance at religious instruction classes, the movement is by no means restricted to this small number. In 1930, these week-day church-schools had been established in 2058 centers spread through forty-five States, the total enrollment being estimated at 260,988 students, the majority of which are conducted by Protestant denominations.[14] There is ample evidence that this number has been substantially increased since the time indicated above.[15] In these cities, the pupils are withdrawn from their school-studies and are taught by special teachers provided by the churches, either in the church-building or in rooms in the school building.[16]

The legality of such an arrangement drawn up between the Board of Education and the parents (without statutory provision) whereby the latter designate the particular religion classes which they wish their children to attend has been tested in New York and Wisconsin. The basis of complaint has been: (1) That such an arrangement is in violation of the State Constitutions[17] which prohibits the use of public property or money in aid or maintenance of any school or institution of learning which is under the control of any religious denomination; (2) and of the education law which requires that

[12] *Oregon Code Annotated* (1930), § 3501.

[13] *Illinois School Laws* (ed. by S. S. DuHamel), 1932, Chap. II, § 7, p. 14.

[14] *Recent Social Trends*, II, 1036.

[15] Gorham, *A Study of the Status of Week-day Church Schools in the United States*, 1934.

[16] *Recent Social Trends*, I, 370.

[17] *Constitution of New York*, Art. 9, Sec. 4; *Constitution of Wisconsin*, Art. 1, Sec. 18.

pupils "shall regularly attend upon instruction for the entire time during which the schools . . . are in session." [18]

In New York, the practice was first submitted to the court in the case of Stein v. Brown in June, 1925 [19] in which Stein asked the court to grant an injunction restraining Brown and other members of the Board of Education of the City of Mount Vernon from permitting students in the public schools to be excused from school for forty-five minutes once a week for instruction in the churches. In this case cards were printed by the school-press as an exercise for industrial-arts students; and the teachers in the public schools also had to check the attendance during the time for which they were paid to teach. The court, in granting the injunction, held that neither the State nor any subdivision thereof could use its property, funds, or credit in aid of a school wholly or in part under the control of any religious denomination; and that the practice of excusing the pupils from school for religious instruction was unlawful. However, the last part of this decision was overruled on May 10, 1927, in the case of People *ex rel.* Lewis v. Graves.[20] In this case Lewis applied to the court for an order of peremptory mandamus to compel Graves, the Commissioner of Education, to stop the practice whereby the school authorities of the City of White Plains allowed pupils from the ages of seven to fourteen to attend religious instruction one day during the week for a period of one-half hour. In this case no public money was used to aid the religion classes, although some time was required of the public school teachers to register and check up on attendance. The court held that this practice was not a diversion of public funds sufficient to constitute a violation of the State Constitution. And in as much as a child, otherwise regular in attendance at school, could be excused to take instruction in music or dancing, the amount of time conceded to attend religion classes was not sufficient to constitute an infringement of the school attendance law. In the opinion which was concurred in by Chief Justice Cardozo, the court stated:

[18] *Educational Law of New York State* (1931), Sec. 621.

[19] 211 N. Y. S. 822.

[20] 156 N. E. 663.

> The separation of the public school system from a denominational institution is thus complete. Jealous sectaries may view with alarm the introduction in the schools of religious teaching, which to the unobservant eye is but faintly tinted with denominationalism. Eternal vigilance is the price of constitutional rights. But it is impossible to say, as a matter of law, that the slightest infringement of constitutional right or abuse of statutory requirement has been shown in this case.

In Wisconsin, cards asking that children be excused from school one hour each week to receive religious instruction were handed to pupils by the teachers, signed by the parents, returned to the teachers, sorted by them, and passed on to the ministers of the churches designated. The Attorney-General ruled that public money was being used for religious purposes or for teaching sectarian doctrines in public schools in violation of the State Constitution.[21] However, he also stated that it is within the power of school boards to excuse pupils for any reasonable period provided that, in the instance of religious instruction, the teachers have no part and no school machinery be used for that purpose. The result of this latter is that provisions could be made for religious instruction, if the parents and the churches completely supervise the arrangement.

An analysis of the reasons given both for and against the legality of such provisions indicates that the decision ultimately rested on the viewpoint of the court itself. If it was influenced by the exaggerated separatist policy which looks with horror on any identification of religious instruction with the public-school system, the decisions were opposed to any plan; if a more balanced and tolerant position was taken, the plan was upheld. And wherever court action is taken in this regard, no matter what the technicalities of the case might be, it is safe to say that the decision will always be determined by whatever attitude the court may have.

Public opinion, however, has been changing considerably in the United States during the past decade, since the consequences of a godless education are so strikingly evident in American life. Because of the appalling increase in crime the need has been recognized

[21] *Opinions of the Attorney-General of Wisconsin* (1926), XV, 483-488.

for a *thorough* religious education of the youth. The following quotation from an address delivered by the Hon. Alfred J. Talley, Former Judge, Court of General Sessions, New York City, illustrates how the need of such instruction is being recognized: [22]

> A few years ago, so distinguished an educator as the President of Columbia University, for whose opinions and whose courage I have the very highest respect, at the opening of Columbia's 182nd academic year, deplored the shortcomings of deficiencies of modern schooling. Referring to the unhappy prevalence of crime, he is reported as having said: "If the manifestations of individual temperament and character, personal and social, which confront us day by day are the result of what we are accustomed to call education, then something pretty serious is the matter with that education." President Butler is not reported as having said what that "pretty serious matter" was, but we will say so tonight. He only went so far as to add that the one true test of education is its effect upon character and conduct.
>
> More than ten years ago the judges of the Court of General Sessions in New York, the oldest Court in the United States and the greatest criminal court in the world, sat in serious conference and asked themselves "What is the matter?" They were trained men, face to face daily with the tremendous responsibility of dealing with serious crimes from murder down. . . . Their answer to themselves was put in the form of an unsolicited public statement to which some prominence was given and which created more than passing notice.
>
> It was signed on behalf of the Bench by three of the judges, of whom I was one. They were representatives of the Protestant, Jewish, and Catholic faiths, and they stated that, in their judgment, *the main and outstanding cause of the criminality which was then and is today unhappily a disgrace of America, was the indifference of our people to the need of daily religious teaching to the American child.* Today, ten years later, I have had no reason to change that opinion, nor have my former associates on the Bench changed theirs. That I say to the President of Columbia University is the "something pretty serious" that is the

[22] *Proceedings of the Governor's Conference on Crime, the Criminal and Society* (1935), pp. 89-91.

matter with the education of today and, until that lack is supplied, nothing of lasting benefit will be accomplished.

I can hear it being said, "Oh, yes, but under our laws and Constitution that is a very difficult matter to contend with." Of course it is, but we are in Albany tonight, Governor Lehman, to discuss difficulties and meet them, not to applaud platitudes. It is a difficult matter to stand before the world as the most lawless nation on the face of the earth. That we are. And I say that in this glorious country of ours, with the priceless privilege of liberty that we enjoy, there is less excuse for us being lawless than there is for any nation of the old world. It is a difficult thing for this great Empire State of ours to stagger under a burden of paying more than a million dollars every thirty days to maintain our institutions for delinquents alone. Why is it not time to make a fresh start? You know as well as I do why, in the evolution of policy of this State, religion is kept out of the schools. It came about because, unhappily, one religion was so fearful that another religion would get an advantage that the cowardly and fatal course was adopted of wiping out religious teaching altogether. Pagan divinities and their amours may be glorified—Nero, Caesar, Hannibal, Napoleon, Henry the Eighth—with all their human frailities, their wars and devastations may be expounded and discussed, but the Almighty Father, the Divine Architect, the Merciful Creator who holds the destiny of the American people in the hollow of His hand must not be mentioned before an American child in an American school. Why is it not time to make a fresh start?

. . . I am hopeful, as a result of the Governor's conference, that the permanent Committee will collate and examine the various suggestions made during these conferences. To such Committee I propose the following as a definite and concrete plan:

First: I propose that one-half hour at the opening of school on every day be given to a prescribed course in religion.

Second: That the children be divided into classes, in accordance with the request of the parents, as to the particular religion in which they are to be instructed.

Third: That the instruction be given not by a Minister, Priest, or Rabbi, but by the regular members of the teaching staff, who have passed tests prescribed by the Board of Regents and whose eligibility to take such examinations

> has been certified by the authorities of the respective faiths.
>
> Fourth: If there be children whose parents object to their being placed in any of the three major divisions, that such children be given a prescribed course in ethics.

In an address given at the Attorney-General's Conference on Crime (held in Washington in December, 1934) Kenyon J. Scudder, Chief Probation Officer, Los Angeles County, California, analyzed some of the "Social Aspects of Crime Prevention." His facts were drawn from a study of fourteen thousand Juvenile Court cases in Los Angeles County. In part, he stated:

> Of the fourteen thousand cases studied, only thirty-two per cent were connected with any religious organization, leaving sixty-eight per cent with no connection with any church or religious group. The Catholics and the Jews look after their children.
>
> The Protestant church, which for years has professed its interest and concern over the weak and helpless, has almost turned its back on these unfortunate children . . .[23]

Several deductions may be made from these statements, but the significant one is this—that religious instruction does have a recognized place in the prevention of crime.

In an address to the Protestant Teachers' Association of New York City on February 14, 1937, the well-known Protestant divine, Harry Emerson Fosdick, advocated and endorsed the plan of releasing children from school for religious instruction. Dr. Fosdick declared, in part:

> A complete education involves religion. Surely, one way or another in a country and city like this, we must find the means, even while we keep the Church and State separate, of giving the boys and girls of the nation an opportunity to become acquainted with, possessed by, the great character-producing faiths of our race.
>
> . . . We must be deeply dissatisfied with what is happening to childhood now. Whether one thinks of our economic life, where in this powerful and really opulent country it is so shamefully difficult to drive out even an

[23] *Proceedings of the Attorney-General's Conference on Crime,* p. 416.

> obvious abomination like child labor, whether one thinks of those terrible under-privileged areas of iniquity in our great cities from which comes the great mass of our criminality, whether one thinks of the failure of our home life, the inadequacy of our churches in dealing with education, we must be deeply and penitently dissatisfied.
>
> It is a great thing to be a school teacher. And when now you come, you the teachers of our public schools, and lift your strong united voice, saying, "A complete education involves religion," I think that one of the most important and encouraging things happening in our time.[24]

Benjamin Veit, Assistant Superintendent of Schools in New York City, spoke in a similar vein to the Jewish Teacher Association:

> I urge all of you to give the problem of religious instruction great thought. I do not want to say at this time whether an hour for religious training should be given during school hours or after school, but lend your support to those working for a solution. Work with those who feel that a democracy cannot persist unless there are spiritual values imbibed by children while they are still young.[25]

The Department of Superintendence of the National Educational Association gave the following statement at their meeting in 1932:

> Our society today awaits a new integration of knowledge, aspiration and human purpose . . . Until such an integration is forthcoming, the present condition of moral chaos is likely to continue, and the more fundamental problem of education will defy solution. Whether this is a task of the church or some other agency, we cannot say today; but it would seem to be a task that is essentially religious in nature.[26]

It is certain that religious instruction in the public-school system of the United States can be made to harmonize with both the Constitutional and statutory restrictions of the several States. The actual accomplishment, however, will be determined by the ability of an enlightened public opinion, as exemplified in the above quota-

[24] *The New York Times,* Feb. 15, 1937.

[25] *The New York Times,* Feb. 23, 1937.

[26] *Character Education, Tenth Yearbook of the Department of Superintendence of the National Education Association* (1932), p. 23.

tions, to overcome the deeply-rooted tradition of excluding religious instruction from the school. And if it is successful in procuring a thorough instruction for youth in Christian principles, an American Commonwealth of vigor and moral integrity is assured—a nation that has understood the meaning of Christ's dictum:

> Do not think I am come to destroy the law, or the prophets. I am not come to destroy, but to fulfill. (Matt. v. 17.)

SUPPLEMENT III

CONSTITUTION OF THE CONFRATERNITY OF CHRISTIAN DOCTRINE

The following Constitution, having the approval of the Holy See, is for the parish units of the Confraternity of Christian Doctrine. However it may be stated that some modifications seem to be permissible for those parishes where circumstances might prevent complete adaptation.

ARTICLE I. NAME

The name of this organization shall be The Confraternity of Christian Doctrine of ....
Parish ....

ARTICLE II. OBJECT

The objects of this organization shall be:

(a) Religious training of Catholic elementary-school children not attending Catholic schools, in vacation schools and instruction classes during the school year.

(b) Religious instruction of Catholic youths of high-school age not attending Catholic schools, in suitable study clubs and by other successful methods.

(c) Religious study clubs for adult groups; inquiry classes for non-Catholics.

(d) Religious education of children by parents in the home.

Where not cared for by other agencies, the following activities may be undertaken by the Confraternity: missions for children, clubs and classes for immigrant parents, religious correspondence courses.

A religious program in missions on Sundays and holydays of obligation when the priest is not present to say Mass.

Distribution of Catholic literature, especially papers and magazines; maintenance, at the church or assembly hall, of a bookrack containing pamphlets on Catholic doctrine and practice.

Article III. Membership

Section 1. Active Members. Members of the parish who are willing to take active part in the work of the Confraternity, serving at least one hour a week or fifty hours annually, shall be enrolled in one of the following divisions:

(a) *Teachers,* who shall assist priests and Sisters in catechetical work, especially in religious vacation schools and in instruction classes.

(b) *Fishers* (home visitors), who shall make systematic surveys of the parish, encourage children to attend instruction classes and adults to join study clubs, and promote subscription to the diocesan paper.

(c) *Helpers,* who shall provide facilities for classes and clubs, transport teachers and pupils, and assist with preparation of material for religious vacation schools and instruction classes.

(d) *Study-Club Leaders,* who shall conduct religious study clubs for adults and secular high-school students.

Section 2. Associate Members. Members of the parish who cannot take active part in the Confraternity program, but who wish to make a contribution to its support, shall be admitted as *Associate Members.* These may be classified, according to their annual contribution, as *Contributing, Special, Supporting* or *Sustaining Members.*

Section 3. Both Active and Associate Members shall pray daily for the interests of the Confraternity. They shall receive Holy Communion at least once a month.

Article IV. Officers and Organization

Section 1. The Director shall be the pastor, or a priest appointed by him.

Section 2. The Director shall appoint or arrange for the election of the following officers: president, vice-president, secretary, treasurer, and chairman for each of the four divisions of active membership named in Article III, Section 1.

SECTION 3. The Director, the officers and division chairmen shall constitute the Executive Board of the Confraternity.

ARTICLE V. MEETINGS

SECTION 1. The Executive Board of the Confraternity shall meet once a month.

SECTION 2. A minimum of six classes for the training of workers shall be held each year by each of the division chairmen, under the supervision of the Director.

SECTION 3. General meetings of the entire Confraternity membership shall be held at least semi-annually at the call of the Director.

BIBLIOGRAPHY

Sources

Acta Apostolicae Sedis, Romae, 1909-

Acta et Decreta Conciliorum Recentiorum (Coll. Lacensis), 7 vols., Friburgi-Brisgoviae, 1870-1890.

Acta Sanctae Sedis, 41 vols., Romae, 1865-1908.

Bullarium Romanum, Tomus Undecimus, Luxemburgi, 1867.

Bullarii Romani Continuatio, 13 vols., Prati, 1845-1854.

Canones et Decreta Concilii Tridentini, Naples, 1859.

Codex Juris Canonici, Romae, 1918.

Codicis Juris Canonici Fontes, cura Emi. Petri Card. Gasparri editi, 7 vols., Romae, 1926ss.

Collectanea Sacrae Congregationis de Propaganda Fidei, 2 vols., Romae, 1907.

Concilia Provincialia Baltimori Habita ab anno 1829 usque ad annum 1849, Baltimori, 1851.

Concilii Plenarii Baltimorensis I, Acta et Decreta, Baltimorae, 1853.

Concilii Plenarii Baltimorensis II, Acta et Decreta, Baltimorae, 1868.

Concilii Plenarii Baltimorensis Tertii, Acta et Decreta, Baltimorae, 1886.

Concilii Provincialis Portlandensis in Oregon Quarti, Acta et Decreta, Portlandiae, 1932.

Corpus Juris Canonici, Editio Lipsiensis II (Richter-Friedberg), 2 vols., Lipsiae, 1922.

Corpus Juris Civilis, 3 vols., Berolini, 1928-1929, Vol. III; *Novellae Constitutiones*—R. Schoell, opus Schoelli morte interceptum absolvit G. Kroll.

Decretum gratiani emendatum et notationibus illustratum, una cum glossis, Gregorii XIII Pont. Max. iussu editum, 2 vols., Romae, 1852.

Harduin, Jean, *Acta Conciliorum et Epistolae Decretales ac Constitutiones Summorum Pontificum*, 12 vols., Parisiis, 1715.

Hartzheim, J., *Concilia Germaniae*, 11 vols., Coloniae Augustae Agrippinensium, 1759-1790.

Mansi, J., *Sacrorum Conciliorum Nova et Amplissima Collectio*, 53 vols., Paris—Arnheim-Leipzig, 1901-1927.

Migne, J., *Patrologiae Cursus Completus*—Series Latina, 221 vols. (*MPL*), Paris, 1884-1885; *Series Graeca*, 161 vols. (*MPG*), Paris, 1858-1864.

Monumenta Germaniae Historica, Capitularia Regum Francorum, T. I., Hanover, 1816.

Statuta Archidioecesis Sancti Francisci, San Francisco, 1936.

Reference Works

Aertnys-Damen, *Theologia Moralis*, 11 ed., 2 vols., Taurini, 1928.

Ayrinhac, H. A., *General Legislation on the Sacraments in the New Code of Canon Law*, New York-London, 1928.

[Bachofen], Charles Augustine, *A Commentary on the New Code of Canon Law,* 4 ed., 8 vols., St. Louis, 1921-1929.

Ballerini-Palmieri, *Opus Theologicum Morale,* Vol. 7, Prati, 1893.

Bandas, R., *Catechetical Methods,* New York, 1929.

Barrett, J., *A Comparative Study of the Councils of Baltimore and the Code of Canon Law,* Washington, 1932.

Bellarmino, Roberto Cardinale, *Dichiarazione della Dottrina Cristiana,* Romae, 1842.

Beringer, F., and Steinen, Pet. Al., *Die Ablässe, Ihr Wesen und Gebrauch,* 15 ed., 2 vols., Paderborn, 1922.

Blat, A., *Commentarium Textus Codicis Canonici,* Romae, 1921-1927.

Bondini, P. Aloisius, *De Privilegio Exemptionis,* Romae, 1919.

Bouscaren, T. L., *The Canon Law Digest,* Milwaukee, 1934 (*Cumulative Supplement—1935-1936,* Milwaukee, 1936).

Cappello, F., *Tractatus Canonico-Moralis de Sacramentis,* 3 ed., Vol. III (*De Matrimonio*), Romae, 1933.

Catechismo della Dottrina Cristiana Pubblicato per Ordine da Sua Santità P. Pio X, Romae, 1906.

Catechismus ex decreto SS. Concilii Tridentini ad Parochos, Bassani, 1859.

Catechism of Christian Doctrine, Prepared and Prescribed by the Third Council of Baltimore, New York, 1887.

Catechism of the Council of Trent, tr. by J. Donovan, Baltimore.

Catholic Encyclopedia, The, 15 vols., New York, 1907-1922.

Chelodi, J., *Jus de Personis,* 2 ed., Tridentini, 1927.

Cocchi, G., *Commentarium in Codicem Juris Canonici,* 7 vols., Taurini, 1925-1930.

Code of Iowa (1935), Des Moines, 1935.

Compiled Laws of the State of Michigan (1929), Lansing, 1930.

Congressional Record, Vol. 4, pt. 1, Washington, 1876.

Consolidated Laws of New York (1909), New York City, 1909.

DeMeester, A., *Juris Canonici et Juris Canonico-Civilis Compendium,* 3 vols., Brugis, 1921-1928.

De Operibus S. Roberti Bellarmini, Romae, 1930.

Devoti, Joannis, *Institutionum Canonicarum,* Liber IV, Tomus primus, Leodii, 1883.

Dieckmann, H., *Theologia Fundamentalis, De Ecclesia Tractatus Historico-Dogmaticus,* Vol. 1, Freiburg, 1925.

Dupanloup, M., *The Ministry of Catechizing,* tr., London, 1890.

Fanfani, L., *De Jure Parochorum,* Taurini, 1924.

Gasparri, Peter, *Tractatus Canonicus de Matrimonio,* ed. nova, 2 vols., Civitate Vaticana, 1932.

Gatterer, M., and Krus, F., *The Theory and Practice of the Catechism,* tr. by J. B. Culemans, Ratisbon, 1914.

Göbl, Peter, *Geschichte der Katechese im Abendlande,* Kempten, 1880.

Gorham, Donald R., *A Study of the Status of Week-day Church Schools in the U. S.*, Philadelphia, 1934.

Hefele, Carl, *Conciliengeschichte*, 2 ed., 9 vols., Freiburg im Breisgau, 1873-1890.

Hefele, Carl, *History of the Church Councils*, tr. by William R. Clark, 5 vols., Edinburgh, 1896.

Hezard, F., *Histoire du Catéchisme*, Paris, 1900.

Hinschius, P., *System des Katholischen Kirchenrechts*, Vol. 4, Berlin, 1888.

Illinois School Laws, ed. by S. S. DuHamel, 2 ed., Springfield, Ill., 1932.

Joly, Claude, *Traité Historique des Ecoles Episcopales et Ecclesiastiques*, Paris, 1678.

Lehmkuhl, Augustinus, *Theologia Moralis*, 12 ed., Freiburg im Breisgau, 1914.

Lelanne, J. A., *Influence des Pères de l'Eglise sur l'Education Publique pendant les cinq premiers siècles de l'ère Chrétienne*, Paris, 1850.

Liddell-Scott, *Greek-English Lexicon*, New York-Chicago-Cincinnati, 1897.

Mason's Minnesota Statutes (1927), St. Paul, Minn., 1927.

Mayer, F., *Geschichte des Katechumenats und der Katechese*, Kempten, 1868.

McCormick, P. J., *History of Education*, Washington, 1915.

Melo, Antonio, *De Exemptione Regularium*, Washington, 1921.

Meyenberg, A.-Brossart, Ferdinand, *Homiletic and Catechetical Studies*, 2 ed., Ratisbon—Rome, 1914.

Monroe, P., *A Brief Course in the History of Education*, New York-London, 1909.

Moran, William, *The Government of the Church in the First Century*, New York-Cincinnati, 1913.

Muniz, T., *Procedimientos Eclesiasticos*, 2 ed., 3 vols., Sevilla.

North East Law Reports, n. 156.,

New York Supplement, 211.

Noval, Josephus, *Commentarium Codicis Iuris Canonici*, L. IV, *De Processibus*, Romae, 1926.

Official Code of West Virginia (1931), Charlottesville, 1932.

Opinions of the Attorney-General of Wisconsin (1926), Vol. XV, Madison, 1926.

Oregon Code Annotated (1930), Indianapolis, 1930.

Ottaviani, A., *Institutiones Juris Publici Ecclesiastici*, 2 ed., 2 vols., Typis Polyglotis Vaticanis, 1935.

Otten, Bernard J., *A Manual of the History of Dogma*, 2 vols., St. Louis, 1917-1918.

Pallavicino, Sforza, *Istoria del Concilio di Trento*, 3 vols., Napoli, 1853.

Pallottini, *Collectio Resolutionum Sacrae Congregationis Concilii*, 17 vols., Romae, 1868.

Payen, G., *De Matrimonio*, 3 vols., Zi-Ka-Wei, 1928-1929.

Piatus, Montensis, *Praelectiones Juris Regularis*, 2 vols., Tornaci, 1896.

Poulet, Dom Charles-Raemers, S. S., *A History of the Catholic Church*, 2 vols., St. Louis-London, 1935.

Prat, F., *The Theology of St. Paul*, tr. by John L. Stoddard, 2 vols., London, 1933.

Prindiville, R., *The Confraternity of Christian Doctrine*, Philadelphia, 1932.

Probst, Ferdinand, *Geschichte der Katholischen Katechese*, Breslau, 1886.

Proceedings of the Attorney-General's Conference on Crime, Washington, 1934.

Proceedings of the Governor's Conference on Crime, the Criminal and Society, Sept. 30-Oct. 3, 1935, Albany, N. Y., 1935.

Prümmer, D., *Manuale Juris Canonici*, 4 et 5 ed., Friburgi-Brisgoviae, 1927.

Reichel, O. J., *A Complete Manual of Canon Law*, 2 vols., London, 1896.

Report of the President's Research Committee on Social Trends, 2 vols., New York-London, 1933.

Sabetti-Barrett, S.J., *Compendium Theologiae Moralis*, 3 ed., Neo Eboraci, 1924.

Schaff, P.-Wallace, H., *Select Library of Nicene and Post-Nicene Fathers* (second series), 8 vols., New York, 1894.

Schäfer, T., *De Religiosis*, 2 ed., Münster i. W., 1931.

Schmalzgrueber, F., *Jus Ecclesiasticum Universum*, 12 vols., Ingolstadii, 1728.

Statuto della Venerabile Arciconfraternita della Dottrina Cristiana, Roma, 1928.

South Dakota Compiled Laws (1929), Pierre, S. Dak., 1930.

Suarez, E., *De Remotione Parochorum*, Romae, 1931.

Tenth Yearbook of the Department of Superintendence of the National Education Association, 1932.

Ter-Haar, F., *De Matrimoniis Mixtis Eorumque Remediis*, Taurini-Romae, 1931.

Thomas Aquinas, *Summa Theologica*, Romae, 1894-1928.

Vermeersch, A.-Creusen, J., *Epitome Juris Canonici*, 4 ed., 3 vols., Mechliniae, 1930.

Vromant, G., *De Fidelium Associationibus*, Lovanii, 1932.

Wernz, F. X., *Jus Decretalium*, Tomus III, Romae, 1908.

Wernz-Vidal, *Jus Canonicum*, 5 vols., Romae, 1923-1935.

West, Andrew G., *Alcuin and the Rise of the Christian Schools*, New York, 1892.

Wisconsin Statutes (1910), Madison, 1910.

Periodicals

American Ecclesiastical Review (*AER*), Philadelphia, 1889-

Apollinaris, Romae, 1928-

Archiv für Katholisches Kirchenrecht (*AKKR*), Mainz, 1857-

Commentarium pro Religiosis (*CpR*), Romae, 1920-

Homiletic and Pastoral Review, The (*HPR*), New York, 1900-

Irish Ecclesiastical Record, The (IER), Dublin, 1864-

Jus Pontificium (*JP*), Romae, 1921-

La Civiltà Cattolica (Anno 56—1905), Vol. II.

Periodica de re Canonica et Morali, Brugis, 1905-; ab anno 1927: *Periodica de Canonica, Morali, Liturgica.*

ALPHABETICAL INDEX

BIOGRAPHICAL NOTE

RAYMOND JOSEPH JANSEN was born April 4, 1908, at Madelia, Minn. His grammar and high school education was completed at Mater Dolorosa School and the public high school of the same town. He received the degree of Bachelor of Arts from the College of St. Mary's, Winona, Minn., in 1929. In October of the same year he entered the Seminary of the North American College, in Rome, Italy, and was ordained to the priesthood December 8, 1932. His theological studies were made at the University of the Propaganda and the Gregorian University. From the former was obtained the Licentiate Degree in Sacred Theology. In the fall of 1934 he enrolled at the Catholic University of America to pursue a graduate course of studies in Canon Law.

CANON LAW STUDIES

1. Freriks, Rev. Celestine A., C.PP.S., J.C.D., Religious Congregations in Their External Relations, 121 pp., 1916.
2. Galliher, Rev. Daniel M., O.P., J.C.D., Canonical Elections, 117 pp., 1917.
3. Borkowski, Rev. Aurelius L., O.F.M., J.C.D., De Confraternitatibus Ecclesiasticis, 136 pp., 1918.
4. Castillo, Rev. Cayo, J.C.D., Disertacion Historico-Canonica sobre la Potestad del Cabildo en Sede Vacante o Impedida del Vicario Capitular, 99 pp., 1919 (1918).
5. Kubelbeck, Rev. William J., S.T.B., J.C.D., The Sacred Penitentiaria and Its Relation to Faculties of Ordinaries and Priests, 129 pp., 1918.
6. Petrovits, Rev. Joseph, J.C., S.T.D., J.C.D., The New Church Law on Matrimony, X-461 pp., 1919.
7. Hickey, Rev. John J., S.T.B., J.C.D., Irregularities and Simple Impediments in the New Code of Canon Law, 100 pp., 1920.
8. Klekotka, Rev. Peter J., S.T.B., J.C.D., Diocesan Consultors, 179 pp., 1920.
9. Wanenmacher, Rev. Francis, J.C.D., The Evidence in Ecclesiastical Procedure Affecting the Marriage Bond, 1920 (Printed 1935).
10. Golden, Rev. Henry Francis, J.C.D., Parochial Benefices in the New Code, IV-119 pp., 1921 (Printed 1925).
11. Koudelka, Rev. Charles J., J.C.D., Pastors, Their Rights and Duties According to the New Code of Canon Law, 211 pp., 1921.
12. Melo, Rev. Antonius, O.F.M., J.C.D., De Exemptione Regularium, X-188 pp., 1921.
13. Schaaf, Rev. Valentine Theodore, O.F.M., S.T.B., J.C.D., The Cloister, X-180 pp., 1921.
14. Burke, Rev. Thomas Joseph, S.T.D., J.C.D., Competence in Ecclesiastical Tribunals, IV-117 pp., 1922.
15. Leech, Rev. George Leo, J.C.D., A Comparative Study of the Constitution "Apostolicae Sedis" and the "Codex Juris Canonici," 179 pp., 1922.
16. Motry, Rev. Hubert Louis, S.T.D., J.C.D., Diocesan Faculties According to the Code of Canon Law, II-167 pp., 1922.
17. Murphy, Rev. George Lawrence, J.C.D., Delinquencies and Penalties in The Administration and the Reception of the Sacraments, IV-121 pp., 1923.
18. O'Reilly, Rev. John Anthony, S.T.B., J.C.D., Ecclesiastical Sepulture in the New Code of Canon Law, II-129 pp., 1923.
19. Michalicka, Rev. Wenceslas Cyrill, O.S.B., J.C.D., Judicial Procedure in Dismissal of Clerical Exempt Religious, 107 pp., 1923.

20. Dargin, Rev. Edward Vincent, S.T.B., J.C.D., Reserved Cases According to the Code of Canon Law, IV-103 pp., 1924.
21. Godfrey, Rev. John A., S.T.B., J.C.D., The Right of Patronage According to the Code of Canon Law, 153 pp., 1924.
22. Hagedorn, Rev. Francis Edward, J.C.D., General Legislation on Indulgences, II-154 pp., 1924.
23. King, Rev. James Ignatius, J.C.D., The Administration of the Sacraments to Dying Non-Catholics, V-141 pp., 1924.
24. Winslow, Rev. Francis Joseph, O.F.M., J.C.D., Vicars and Prefects Apostolic, IV-149 pp., 1924.
25. Correa, Rev. Jose Servelion, S.T.L., J.C.D., La Potestad Legislativa de la Iglesia Catolica, IV-127 pp., 1925.
26. Dugan, Rev. Henry Francis, A.M., J.C.D., The Judiciary Department of the Diocesan Curia, 87 pp., 1925.
27. Keller, Rev. Charles Frederick, S.T.B., J.C.D., Mass Stipends, 167 pp., 1925.
28. Paschang, Rev. John Linus, J.C.D., The Sacramentals According to the Code of Canon Law, 129 pp., 1925.
29. Pointek, Rev. Cyrillus, O.F.M., S.T.B., J.C.D., De Indulto Exclaustrationis necnon Saecularizationis, XIII-289 pp., 1925.
30. Kearney, Rev. Richard Joseph, S.T.B., J.C.D., Sponsors at Baptism According to the Code of Canon Law, IV-127 pp., 1925.
31. Bartlett, Rev. Chester Joseph, A.M., LL.B., J.C.D., The Tenure of Parochial Property in the United States of America, V-108 pp., 1926.
32. Kilker, Rev. Adrian Jerome, J.C.D., Extreme Unction, V-425 pp., 1926.
33. McCormick, Rev. Robert Emmett, J.C.D., Confessors of Religious, VIII-266 pp., 1926.
34. Miller, Rev. Newton Thomas, J.C.D., Founded Masses According to the Code of Canon Law, VII-93 pp., 1926.
35. Roelker, Rev. Edward G., S.T.D., J.C.D., Principles of Privilege According to the Code of Canon Law, XI-166 pp., 1926.
36. Bakalarczyk, Rev. Richardus, M.I.C., J.U.D., De Novitiatu, VIII-208 pp., 1927.
37. Pizzuti, Rev. Lawrence, O.F.M., J.U.L., De Parochis Religiosis, 1927. (Not Printed.)
38. Bliley, Rev. Nicholas Martin, O.S.B., J.C.D., Altars According to the Code of Canon Law, XIX-132 pp., 1927.
39. Brown, Mr. Brendan Francis, A.B., LL.M., J.U.D., The Canonical Juristic Personality with Special Reference to its Status in the United States of America, V-212 pp., 1927.
40. Cavanaugh, Rev. William Thomas, C.P., J.U.D., The Reservation of the Blessed Sacrament, VIII-101 pp., 1927.
41. Doheny, Rev. William J., C.S.C., A.B., J.U.D., Church Property: Modes of Acquisition, X-118 pp., 1927.
42. Feldhaus, Rev. Aloysius H., C.PP.S., J.C.D., Oratories, IX-141 pp., 1927.

43. Kelly, Rev. James Patrick, A.B., J.C.D., The Jurisdiction of the Simple Confessor, X-208 pp., 1927.
44. Neuberger, Rev. Nicholas J., J.C.D., Canon 6 or the Relation of the Codex Juris Canonici to the Preceding Legislation, V-95 pp. 1927.
45. O'Keefe, Rev. Gerald Michael, J.C.D., Matrimonial Dispensations, Powers of Bishops, Priests, and Confessors, VIII-232 pp., 1927.
46. Quigley, Rev. Joseph A. M., A.B., J.C.D., Condemned Societies, 139 pp., 1927.
47. Zaplotnik, Rev. Johannes Leo, J.C.D., De Vicariis Foraneis, X-142 pp., 1927.
48. Duskie, Rev. John Aloysius, A.B., J.C.D., The Canonical Status of the Orientals in the United States, VIII-196 pp., 1928.
49. Hyland, Rev. Francis Edward, J.C.D., Excommunication, Its Nature, Historical Development and Effects, VIII-181 pp., 1928.
50. Reinmann, Rev. Gerald Joseph, O.M.C., J.C.D., The Third Order Secular of Saint Francis, 201 pp., 1928.
51. Schenk, Rev. Francis J., J.C.D., The Matrimonial Impediments of Mixed Religion and Disparity of Cult, XVI-318 pp., 1929.
52. Coady, Rev. John Joseph, S.T.D., J.U.D., A.M., The Appointment of Pastors, VIII-150 pp., 1929.
53. Kay, Rev. Thomas Henry, J.C.D., Competence in Matrimonial Procedure, VIII-164 pp., 1929.
54. Turner, Rev. Sidney Joseph, C.P., J.U.D., The Vow of Poverty, XLIX-217 pp., 1929.
55. Kearney, Rev. Raymond A., A.B., S.T.D., J.C.D., The Principles of Delegation, VII-149 pp., 1929.
56. Conran, Rev. Edward James, A.B., J.C.D., The Interdict, V-163 pp., 1930.
57. O'Neil, Rev. William H., J.C.D., Papal Rescripts of Favor, VII-218 pp., 1930.
58. Bastnagel, Rev. Clement Vincent, J.U.D., The Appointment of Parochial Adjutants and Assistants, XV-257 pp., 1930.
59. Ferry, Rev. William A., A.B., J.C.D., Stole Fees, V-136, pp., 1930.
60. Costello, Rev. John Michael, A.B., J.C.D., Domicile and Quasi-Domicile, VII-201 pp., 1930.
61. Kremer, Rev. Michael Nicholas, A.B., S.T.B., J.C.D., Church Support in the United States, VI-136 pp., 1930.
62. Angulo, Rev. Luis, C.M., J.C.D., Legislation de la Iglesia sobre la intencion en la application de la Santa Misa, VII-104 pp., 1931.
63. Frey, Rev. Wolfgang, Norbert, O.S.B., A.B., J.C.D., The Act of Religious Profession, VIII-174 pp., 1931.
64. Roberts, Rev. James Brendan, A.B., J.C.D., The Banns of Marriage, XIV-140 pp., 1931.
65. Ryder, Rev. Raymond Aloysius, A.B., J.C.D., Simony, IX-151 pp., 1931.

66. Campagna, Rev. Angelo, Ph.D., J.U.D., Il Vicario Generale del Vescovo, VII-205 pp., 1931.
67. Cox, Rev. Joseph Godfrey, A.B., J.C.D., The Administration of Seminaries, VI-124 pp., 1931.
68. Gregory, Rev. Donald J., J.U.D., The Pauline Privilege, XV-165 pp., 1931.
69. Donohue, Rev. John F., J.C.D., The Impediment of Crime, VII-110 pp., 1931.
70. Dooley, Rev. Eugene A., O.M.I., J.C.D., Church Law on Sacred Relics, IX-143 pp., 1931.
71. Orth, Rev. Clement Raymond, O.M.C., J.C.D., The Approbation of Religious Institutes, 171 pp., 1931.
72. Pernicone, Rev. Joseph M., A.B., J.C.D., The Ecclesiastical Prohibition of Books, XII-267 pp., 1932.
73. Clinton, Rev. Connell, A.B., J.C.D., The Paschal Precept, IX-108 pp., 1932.
74. Donnelly, Rev. Francis B., A.M., S.T.L., J.C.D., The Diocesan Synod, VIII-125 pp., 1932.
75. Torrente, Rev. Camilo, C.M.F., J.C.D., Las Processiones Sagradas, V-145 pp., 1932.
76. Murphy, Rev. Edwin J., C.PP.S., J.C.D., Suspension Ex Informata Conscientia, XI-122 pp., 1932.
77. Mackenzie, Rev. Eric F., A.M., S.T.L., J.C.D., The Delict of Heresy in its Commission, Penalization, Absolution, VII-124 pp., 1932.
78. Lyons, Rev. Avitus E., S.T.B., J.C.D., The Collegiate Tribunal of First Instance, XI-147 pp., 1932.
79. Connolly, Rev. Thomas A., J.C.D., Appeals, XI-195, pp., 1932.
80. Sangmeister, Rev. Joseph V., A.B., J.C.D., Force and Fear as Precluding Matrimonial Consent, V-211, pp., 1932.
81. Jaeger, Rev. Leo A., A.B., J.C.D., The Administration of Vacant and Quasi-Vacant Episcopal Sees in the United States, IX-229 pp., 1932.
82. Rimlinger, Rev. Herbert T., J.C.D., Error Invalidating Matrimonial Consent, VII-79 pp., 1932.
83. Barrett, Rev. John D. M., S.S., J.C.D., A Comparative Study of the Third Plenary Council of Baltimore and the Code, IX-221 pp., 1932.
84. Carberry, Rev. John J., Ph.D., S.T.D., J.C.D., The Juridical Form of Marriage, X-177 pp., 1934.
85. Dolan, Rev. John L., A.B., J.C.D., The Defensor Vinculi, XII, 157 pp., 1934.
86. Hannan, Rev. Jerome D., A.M., S.T.D., LL.B., J.C.D., The Canon Law of Wills, IX-517 pp., 1934.
87. Lemieux, Rev. Delisle A., A.M., J.C.D., The Sentence in Ecclesiastical Procedure, IX-131 pp., 1934.
88. O'Rourke, Rev. James J., A.B., J.C.D., Parish Registers, VII-109 pp., 1934.

89. Timlin, Rev. Bartholomew, O.F.M., A.M., J.C.D., Conditional Matrimonial Consent, X-381 pp., 1934.
90. Wahl, Rev. Francis X., A.B., J.C.D., The Matrimonial Impediments of Consanguinity and Affinity, VI-125 pp., 1934.
91. White, Rev. Robert J., A.B., LL.B., S.T.B., J.C.D., Canonical Ante-Nuptial Promises and the Civil Law, VI-152 pp., 1934.
92. Herrera, Rev. Antonio Parra, O.C.D., J.C.D., Legislacion Ecclesiastica sobra el Ayuno y la Abstinencia, XI-191 pp., 1935.
93. Kennedy, Rev. Edwin J., J.C.D., The Special Matrimonial Process in Cases of Evident Nullity, X-165 pp., 1935.
94. Manning, Rev. John J., A.B., J.C.D., Presumption of Law in Matrimonial Procedure, XI-111 pp., 1935.
95. Moeder, Rev. John M., J.C.D., The Proper Bishop for Ordination and Dimissorial Letters, VII-135 pp., 1935.
96. O'Mara, Rev. William A., A.B., J.C.D., Canonical Causes for Matrimonial Dispensations, IX-155 pp., 1935.
97. Reilly, Rev. Peter, J.C.D., Residence of Pastors, IX-81 pp., 1935.
98. Smith, Rev. Mariner T., O.P., S.T.Lr., J.C.D., The Penal Law for Religious, VII-169 pp., 1935.
99. Whalen, Rev. Donald W., A.M., J.C.D., The Value of Testimonial Evidence in Matrimonial Procedure, XIII-297 pp., 1935.
100. Cleary, Rev. Joseph F., J.C.D., Canonical Limitations on the Alienation of Church Property, VIII-141 pp., 1936.
101. Glynn, Rev. John C., J.C.D., The Promoter of Justice, XX-337 pp., 1936.
102. Brennan, Rev. James H., S.S., M.A., S.T.B., J.C.L., The Simple Convalidation of Marriage.
103. Brunini, Rev. Joseph Bernard, J.C.L., The Clerical Obligations of Canons 139 and 142.
104. Connor, Rev. Maurice, A.B., J.C.L., The Administrative Removal of Pastors.
105. Guilfoyle, Rev. Merlin Joseph, J.C.L., Custom.
106. Hughes, Rev. James Austin, A.B., A.M., J.C.L., Witnesses in Criminal Trials of Clerics.
107. Jansen, Rev. Raymond J., A.B., S.T.L., J.C.L., Canonical Provisions for Catechetical Instruction.
108. Kealy, Rev. John James, A.B., J.C.L., The Introductory Libellus in Church Court Procedure.
109. McManus, Rev. James Edward, C.SS.R., J.C.L., The Administration of Temporal Goods in Religious Institutes.
110. Moriarity, Rev. Eugene James, J.C.L., Oaths in Ecclesiastical Courts.
111. Rainer, Rev. Eligius George, C.SS.R., J.C.L., Suspension of Clerics.
112. Reilly, Rev. Thomas F., C.SS.R., J.C.L., Visitation of Religious.

www.ingramcontent.com/pod-product-compliance
Lightning Source LLC
LaVergne TN
LVHW050223080826
844660LV00012B/460

* 9 7 8 0 8 1 3 2 2 2 9 6 7 *